To Julie & Roger

Thank you for happy
memories

Galya & Roni

13.07.2017

P.S.

Some more good ideas

ABOVE Weatherproof wicker, fabric, and rugs bring indoor comforts to outdoor living spaces. Wherever you have seating, you'll want to be sure the floor is level for the safety of those both walking and sitting.

LEFT Build a platform up to an elevated deck to avoid that awkward, leggy look. Planting beds and stone retaining walls give a lift to this second-level deck, while the curved design breaks the house's straight lines.

patios

● ● ● FOR ONE-STORY HOUSES OR THOSE THAT offer access to the backyard through a ground-level exit, a patio can pave the way to the outdoors. The good news is that designing an outdoor living space is easier and less expensive than adding on an interior one. Basically, all you need is the floor and you're ready to start furnishing. Of course, that means the style of patio surface you choose is an important one. Plus, a patio—especially a costly one made of mortared stone or cement—should be considered a permanent feature in the landscape.

Start by looking at all the materials available for surfacing your outdoor floor. What you choose should blend with your surroundings, including the style of your home and other materials used in the landscape. Would you consider your home and landscape formal in design? If so, classic brick or pavers might be the answer for you. For a more rustic environment, natural flagstone would better match the mood.

Ground-level patios don't have to be pricey to be both pretty and practical. Pea gravel held in place by edging and plant life makes a suitable surface that only needs occasional raking to keep it looking good.

LEFT Flagstone can be mortared or dry-laid, depending on how durable and permanent you want your patio to be. Mortared flagstone such as this should be installed on a poured or crushed cement base and is more costly to create than a dry-laid option.

ABOVE Concrete pavers are more dye-friendly than ever before, allowing them to be made in a wider range of shapes and colors. Pavers are even being tumbled out to mimic charming cobblestones.

LEFT Limestone and travertine are building materials that have been used since ancient times. Now, tiles and pavers cut from these natural stones are bringing classic elegance to homes in all climates.

• patio materials

Besides looks (and cost, of course), consider the best surface for the intended use of your patio. For outdoor dining and entertainment areas, solid, level surfaces such as those created by slate, poured concrete, or pavers would be best. No matter what you choose to top off your new patio, don't forget to get the foundation right. For most surfaces, you'll need to excavate a level area, then smooth out a base of crushed gravel topped with sand. Brick, pavers, and stone can be set into sand only (dry-laid) or mortared into a cement pad (wet-laid).

If you live in a cold climate, the proper foundation is critical to prevent heaving, when water freezes under the surface of the paving, forcing it to push up in areas. This can be caused by improper drainage material under the patio or by laying the paving product over an expansive soil like clay without drainage material.

Cement remains the most widely used patio material, staying at the top of the list because of its relative affordability and endless versatility. Cement or cement pavers can be tinted, stamped, or scored into many looks, or cut into colored tiles of any size.

Molded concrete paving slabs are manufactured to be almost as strong as stone. This patio demonstrates how modern and clean cement can be in its natural state and how well it combines with any architecture, even very traditional.

A classic brick patio warmly complements most architectural styles and materials. When held in place with sturdy edging—like the low side walls of this lush courtyard—and set correctly into sand or crushed gravel, a brick patio will last for years.

more about...
PATIO MATERIALS

onsider the style you want and the budget you have before you purchase patio materials. Here is a list of the most common products available, listed in order from least to most costly:

- Easy for the do-it-yourselfer, **pea and crushed gravel** is a good choice for the budget-conscious landscaper. This informal material accommodates curves and demands little more maintenance than the occasional raking. Gravel comes with color choices, including black, white, and earthy browns and reds. Most patios require edging to keep the pebbles in place. For those who live in a cold climate, consider that loose gravel isn't easy to shovel. If you need to use the walkway when the snow flies, another option is best.

- Manufacturers are having a lot more design fun with **concrete** these days. A poured concrete patio can be scored, tinted, and stamped, so it can be used to create clean, modern patios or rustic ones that mimic stone. Cut concrete is available in small, interlocking pavers or large steppers that don't require mortar to stay put.

Concrete pavers are as tough as brick but are lighter weight, less costly, and offered in more colors, shapes, and styles.

- Whether mortared in place or dry-laid over a smooth, level base of gravel or stone dust, **clay-fired brick** is a durable material that holds up better than the others in cold climates. Brick is relatively easy to install, and can be laid out in a variety of interesting patterns.

- It's hard to beat the earthy beauty of **natural stone**. The most common (and durable) is flagstone, which comes in a variety of shapes and shades. Natural flagstone can be dry-laid like pieces in a puzzle or cut into uniform squares and mortared in place. Either way, once in place, flagstone demands little maintenance to look great.

- The uniform geometric shapes and clean edges of **ceramic and stone tile** create a smooth and durable patio surface. The tile you choose should be designed for outdoor use in your climate. Shop for terra-cotta, machine-made quarry, molded paver, or synthetic-stone tile.

more patio ideas

ABOVE Flagstone can be cut to create graceful patio shapes to counter the squared-off lines of a house. These flat stone pieces create a smooth walking surface, especially when installed on level substrate.

RIGHT Natural edgings help blur the lines between a straight-edged patio and its surroundings. Stone steps, flagstone, and large boulders mix it up with a brick pad, conjuring the beauty of an outdoor amphitheater.

ABOVE One advantage of a patio? You can carve out a place to gather on most any level spot in your yard. Sheltered by fast-growing bamboo and trees at the back of a property, this inexpensive pea gravel pad is ready to party.

ABOVE Natural flagstone goes together like pieces of a puzzle. When they're set into a 3-inch or deeper bed of sand or gravel, the stones will stay in place.

RIGHT Brick is a classic patio material thanks to it's versatility and all-weather strength. This patio is designed to punctuate a large yard and to highlight the owner's favorite collectible . . . an antique millstone.

patio coverings

● ● ● TO MAKE YOUR PATIO MORE INVITING AT ALL hours of the day, consider topping it with a shade-making pergola. By definition, a pergola is an open-air structure consisting of posts supporting an open roof of girders and cross rafters. Though pergolas have surged in popularity lately, they've actually been around since ancient times and were a common feature in early Renaissance gardens.

Pergolas add a pretty structural component to a backyard, especially when softened with trained vines. Shade, intimacy, and privacy are the most important benefits of a pergola. Depending on the site and house style, a pergola can be attached to the house or designed as a freestanding structure.

A custom pergola can be attached to the back of the house to turn a patio into a more inviting porch retreat. With square posts and an open roof of girders and narrow cross rafters, this structure falls within the classic definition of a pergola.

BELOW Tuck girders under the back eaves to tie a pergola seamlessly to your house. Here, the eaves are extended to partially cover the stone tile patio, creating more shelter, and then they become open rafters.

ABOVE Create your own storybook structure with garden department timbers. Lacy lattice sections soften this pergola's support posts and offer up a spot for vines to grow and eventually add more shade to the garden rest stop.

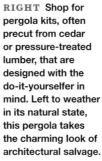

RIGHT Shop for pergola kits, often precut from cedar or pressure-treated lumber, that are designed with the do-it-yourselfer in mind. Left to weather in its natural state, this pergola takes the charming look of architectural salvage.

porches

● ● ● IN SOME CLIMATES—WHERE THE SUN IS harsh or the bugs are tireless—it makes sense to take the deck concept to the next step by adding a fixed roof and screened walls. This added protection allows you to enjoy your space more often if you keep sun, wind, bugs, and rain at bay. Add a roof over both raised or ground-level decks, but keep in mind that structural coverings add weight and have their own requirements for the proper foundations and supports.

A covered back porch also allows you to pack in a few more comforts you enjoy inside your dwelling, including cushioned furniture, lighting, and electric fans—almost anything that can't be exposed to the elements. Think about how you want to use this type of outdoor room. Entertaining friends regardless of weather? Dining alfresco to all hours of the night? Reading by lamplight or even watching television? Make sure you build in plenty of floor space for all the relaxation you dream of; homeowners often regret not making a porch space bigger, but never not making it smaller.

A simple, shed-roof porch addition—especially when screened in—is a comfortable way to enjoy your garden and catch shady breezes. This cozy porch was built on top of the raised patio to bring the screen door in line with the windows.

LEFT Create a zone between structures, such as a breezeway between house and garage, to make the space more usable. Asymmetrical lattice and a pale blue ceiling turn on the porch charm in this connecting space.

ABOVE Why stop at a plain wooden deck when you can create a porch ambience by adding a slant roof and sturdy pillars. A porch is more visually integrated with the architecture, especially a wraparound such as this country example.

LEFT Look to the niches created by exterior bump-outs to find protected areas for a back porch. Smooth poured cement lays out ample floor space under the quaint rafters of this sitting area.

paths and walkways

●●● FROM A PRACTICAL POINT OF VIEW, BACKYARD paths and walkways get you from one place to another in a landscape plan. Successful paths are smooth, well-defined, and—for nighttime safety—amply lit. Aesthetically speaking, these footpaths can visually link the elements of your yard and underscore your architecture and other hardscape elements. Even more, a wandering walkway can add to the experience of traversing your landscape while leading visitors to its highlights.

Whether you need a design that takes people directly where they need to go or is gently curving and meandering, you have many options for laying down a functional and attractive walkway. Many are prime projects for a do-it-yourselfer.

ABOVE Border a garden bed with 18-inch pavers to create a path and mowing strip in one. Dug-in flush with the ground, this path is easy to mow.

ABOVE Large sections of flagstone make a natural walkway wide enough for two. Here, one section is used to bridge a small, manufactured creek that recycles water and babbles all day.

PERFECTING THE PATHWAY

t he best width for a path depends on what kind of path it is. A primary walkway leads from a garage or driveway to an exterior door or through a side yard from the front yard to back. Another type of primary path leads from a back door to a patio or deck, when you'll be carrying grilling equipment and other entertaining necessities. Think about level materials that won't shift, such as concrete, brick, or pavers, for this main artery.

Secondary paths are connectors meant for lone pedestrians who aren't carrying groceries, pushing a lawnmower, or controlling a dog on a leash, for instance. Gravel, mulch, and other loose materials are adequate for this type of walkway.

Here are some guidelines for both types:

• 18 inches is a minimum width for a secondary walkway;

• 24 inches is a minimum width for a primary path, but 36 inches is standard;

• 48 inches is a comfortable width for two people.

Use a mix of materials to create a more alluring walkway. This path to the back door contains a mix of gravel, cement tiles, flagstone steppers, and a center medallion that offers a spot to slow down and enjoy the journey.

more pathway ideas

Vary the width or direction of the path for an interesting look. Staggered slate tiles add even more dimension to this path, giving it a casual feel.

ABOVE When held tightly within the strips of edging, crushed gravel settles into a firm and level walkway with adequate drainage. Choose crushed gravel over pea gravel because it packs more firmly, especially if you purchase the "dust" or "fines" with the crushed pieces that settle into air pockets.

TOP Brick pathways can add traditional beauty for years even without mortar. This path and arbor would feel more formal if the brick had been set in mortar and not allowed grass to grow in the joints. It's just right, though, leading to this lush cottage garden.

ABOVE A narrow pathway can break up the various elements and garden beds in the yard, making sure the greenery forms distinct areas of landscaping. This intimate path makes guests feel as though they are walking directly through the garden.

• steps
and stairs

Not all back lawns are as even as a golf course. If your personal outback includes hills, inclines, or multiple-level living areas, think about how steps can help access more usable space and boost its livability.

Like walkways, steps play a practical role by offering smooth and safe passage to a particular area such as a deck, patio, porch, or exterior entryway. For these situations, repeating materials, such as brick or wood, from your home's architecture or deck design results in a seamless look. Smooth poured-cement stairs are a top choice, but an expensive one due to the labor involved.

For a naturalized look, consider flagstone, fieldstone, stack stone, pavers, and timber—or a combination of these. Though you should always check with local codes when building steps, generally you aren't required to have handrails with four or less risers. If space and the degree of incline or decline allow, design flat walkways between a series of steps for a more inviting walk space than a steep stairway.

Steps manufactured to mimic all types of stones are strong but not as heavy as the real thing. These granite look-alikes are incorporated into a gravel walkway to ease the climb on this incline.

LEFT Make reaching a second-level deck an enjoyable journey with plantings and interesting railings. The terraced planting beds make these steps feel a little more "planted in" to the landscape.

ABOVE On gently sloping properties, folding a few steps into a walkway will make the climb easier for visitors. This brick walkway is broken up by a couple of stone steps that are safely visible.

LEFT The right steps can help turn a tough-to-navigate area in your yard into a real walk in the park. In this sloping side yard, neatly cut paving tiles and natural-edge manufactured steps take visitors comfortably through a white garden.

softening paths and patios

● ● ● ENGLISH GARDENERS REFER TO PATIOS, pathways, and other hardscape elements as the "bones" of their gardens and often regard them as invitations to plant. Softening the structure of a deck, patio, or porch with small trees, shrubs, flowers, and edibles instantly gives your yard a more evolved, natural look. Similarly, mixed annual or perennial beds outlining patios or pathways add color and personality (not to mention fragrance and touchable texture) to these transition areas, spaces that can otherwise seem stark or disconnected from the environment. If you're building walls, look for alpine or rock garden plants that happily root in the crooks and crannies of stone elements, allowing foliage and flowers to tumble over them.

Regardless of your hardscape elements, make sure you note the size and growing habits of the plants you choose, to ensure they won't overgrow and impede the structures or walkways. Be mindful of any plants that are messy, including those that drop leaves, fruit, or prickly pods.

RIGHT Natural flagstone leaves small gaps that are perfect for planting hardy, low-growing plants. Flanked by long-blooming perennials such as daisies and daylilies, this softly curving path extends a gracious invitation.

TOP FAR RIGHT Install a single-width footpath for secondary walkways. These flagstones are installed flush to the ground for easy mowing, and lead to a charming focal point, a gated arbor.

BOTTOM FAR RIGHT Plant up to and around a raised deck or patio to make it look nestled into its location. The only breaks in the softly colored flowerbeds make way for steps.

more about...
FOOT-FRIENDLY PLANTS

t here are a number of ground covers that hold up well underfoot. Select one of these to plant alongside backyard walkways or busy patios. Or plant the tougher varieties in the cracks and crevices of brick or stone paths and patios or surrounding retaining walls.

COMMON NAME	BOTANICAL NAME	ZONES
FOR MODERATE TO HEAVY FOOT TRAFFIC		
Blue star creeper	*Pratia pedunculata*, syn. *Lobelia pedunculata*	5–7
Brass buttons	*Leptinella squalida* and cvs., syn. *Cotula squalida*	4–7
Creeping Jenny	*Lysimachia nummularia* and cvs.	4–8
Creeping speedwell	*Veronica repens* and cvs.	5–9
'Doone Valley' thyme	*Thymus* 'Doone Valley'	6–9
Labrador violet	*Viola labradorica*	2–8
Mazus	*Mazus reptans* and cvs.	5–8
Miniature moneywort	*Lysimachia japonica* 'Minutissima'	6–9
Mother-of-thyme	*Thymus serphyllum* and cvs.	4–9
Prostrate speedwell	*Veronica prostrata* and cvs.	5–8
Pussy toes	*Antennaria dioica* and cvs.	5–9
Siberian barren strawberry	*Waldsteinia ternata*	3–8
Spring cinquefoil	*Potentilla neumanniana* and cvs., syn. *P. verna*	5–8
Turkish veronica	*Veronica liwanensis*	4–9
Woolly thyme	*Thymus pseudolanuginosus*	5–9
FOR LIGHT FOOT TRAFFIC		
Alpine lady's mantle	*Alchemilla alpina*	3–8
Baby's tears	*Soleirolia soleirolii* and cvs.	10–11
Beach strawberry	*Fragaria chiloensis*	5–9
'Blue Haze' acaena	*Acaena* 'Blue Haze', syn. *A.* 'Pewter'	7–9
Carpet bugleweed	*Ajuga reptans* and cvs.	3–9
Corsican mint	*Mentha requienii*	6–9
Dwarf mondo grass	*Ophiopogon japonicus* cvs.	7–10
Dwarf wallflower	*Erysimum kotschyanum*	6–8
Goldenstar	*Chrysogonum virginianum* and cvs.	5–8
Irish moss	*Sagina subulata*	4–7
'Kewensis' wintercreeper	*Euonymus fortunei* 'Kewensis'	5–9
Lady's mantle	*Alchemilla ellenbeckii*	6–8
Roman chamomile	*Chamaemelum nobile*	6–9
Serbian bellflower	*Campanula poscharskyana* and cvs.	4–7
Snow-in-summer	*Cerastium tomentosum*	3–7

•container gardens

Container gardens make easy companions for patios and decks. Available in all heights and shapes, vessels filled with plant life offer a needed counterpart to these horizontal surfaces. Use them to fill in blank corners or silhouette them against exterior siding or railings for a more inviting and interesting outdoor space. They also offer the opportunity for spots of color on what is typically a monochromatic surface.

For a fun and foolproof way to design your own garden in a pot, take the container you want to plant to the nursery—or buy plants and planters together. Play around with the different plants until you have an arrangement that has a pleasing color palette and various heights. Remember to factor in how much the plants will grow during the season. Match plants that have similar sunlight and water requirements to help ensure all the plants remain vigorous throughout the season.

ABOVE Think about how much time you have to devote to keeping a container alive and looking good before you decide what to plant. This succulent dish garden is a busy person's dream.

FACING PAGE TOP Blur the straight edges of a patio by placing containers within, across, and outside the perimeter. Here, chaise longues are set on the diagonal to further break up the square lines.

FACING PAGE BOTTOM LEFT Use color to link your containers visually, considering the color of both the plants and planters. Glazed blue pots of different sizes hold a mix of easy-care succulent plants with blue-green hues for a serene back-door welcome.

FACING PAGE BOTTOM RIGHT A large container can anchor an arrangement of multiple planters or hold its own. For visual balance, your plantings should grow to at least one-third of the container's height.

more about...
ARRANGING CONTAINER VIGNETTES

- **Arrange containers in a triangular grouping** in an odd number, which represents a form that is a staple of art and design. Pull together a dominant central element, then flank it with smaller items.

- **Start with the largest container** placed at the rear of the composition and let the others fall to either side, overlapping a bit so the grouping reads as one unit.

- **The more containers you have**, the more triangles you create, remembering the odd number rule. If you want a formal feeling, arrange containers in a symmetrical or balanced grouping. Leave uneven spaces between plants for an asymmetrical, casual look.

planting
the backyard

PLANTINGS LITERALLY BRING A BACKYARD TO LIFE, COUNTERING HARD surfaces and straight lines with soft silhouettes and fresh color. Not just pretty faces, though, flowers and foliage can be trained into privacy screens, garden rooms, or any number of hardworking elements. Or consider how trees and shrubs clean the air and provide shade while adding dimension to your grounds. One of the growing trends in backyards is the edible garden . . . planting schemes that taste as good as they look.

Clearly more than eye candy, plant life tickles other senses, too. Gardens bring touchable texture, intoxicating fragrance, the quiet sounds of leaves on a breeze, and the birds and the bees . . . all of which will lure you out back to enjoy your private getaway.

Borrow some tried-and-true design fundamentals to turn a barren backyard into a lush landscape. Plant a palette of flowers that extends the colors from inside your home for visual flow. Use tall shrubs or dwarf trees of varying heights for dimension and texture. Or add a row of swaying grasses for design rhythm and a sense of calm and order. Create a focal point fountain, garden bed or seating area to pull the eye—and then the visitor—to certain areas.

Rely on these principles to pull together a terrain that offers comfort, color, and intrigue. Plants can do all of that for you and then some.

Layer your backyard with flowering perennials and shrubs for more privacy, interest, and color. Plants also delineate different living areas within the backyard. Stepping stones serve as both edging and a pathway in this California garden, leading visitors on a meandering tour.

dividing up the landscape

● ● ● A SUCCESSFUL LANDSCAPE HAS MULTIPLE areas of interest while appearing as a unified whole. One way to get there is to think about how you arrange the interior elements of your home, and then translate those ideas out back.

Inside, furniture is arranged into tight-knit groupings that direct the flow of traffic through rooms. Area rugs are used to visually pull together the arrangement and add color or pattern. Statement pieces create focal points and anchor the area. Art and accessories fill in, adding personality and interest.

Outside, patios and decks in all materials and shapes act like area rugs. They don't have to hug tightly to houses and property lines, but can be laid out in any quadrant of your plot for a more welcoming design. Think of trees as focal points. Arrange shrubs or fencing to delineate areas like interior walls do—to guide foot traffic and create a sense of discovery that doesn't happen when you experience a space all at once.

Extend a patio's reach—and sense of welcome—by laying out a soft boundary of low-growing plants. The clean lines of this terraced patio step down to concrete edging that surrounds a fine gravel pathway and a bed of drought-resistant succulents.

ABOVE A well-organized backyard can host more hobbies than you think. Rows of trees and tidy gardens with roses, boxwoods, and other formal plants direct the way to a soccer field via a flagstone walkway.

LEFT Raised flowerbeds are easier on the back and double as privacy buffers that are half wall and half growing things. A little-used side yard gets pulled into the fun with chic and simple concrete elements—pavers and poured concrete beds and built-ins.

planted solutions

● ● ● OUTDOOR LIVING SPACES CAN SUPPORT any after-hours pursuits you have in mind…from grilling for friends to napping in the shade. Filling out those spaces with plant life will add another layer of pleasure. Just think about that nap without the shade tree!

Use flowers and foliage to knit your house with its natural surroundings. Foundation plantings, for instance, will soften and color the stark angles between house and turf. A border of boxwoods can become a living partial wall between a dining patio and yard.

Plants also extend the mood and style of your interiors to the outside. A tumble of cottage blooms in a loose English garden suggests casual romance. On the other hand, a carefully trimmed hedge and statuary carry out an air of formality.

Think about how you want your yard to function and feel before you head out to the nursery to purchase plants. Impulse buys can lead to a disjointed garden. Instead, plan a garden that flows beautifully from inside the house and around the main living elements of your yard.

Plant a deep border of mixed greens along a fence line to soften an outdoor room's backdrop. Screened for privacy and partially covered, this space has the comfort of an open-air family room.

more about...
CALL BEFORE
YOU DIG.

there are a staggering number of underground utilities that snake beneath our yards and homes. Due to soil erosion and other typography changes, some lines can exist inches below the surface. Hitting or severing a line can mean injury to you or an interruption of service to you and your neighbors. And you may be held responsible for the cost of repairs.

It's easy to avoid the gamble. A federally mandated, national "Call Before You Dig" number—811—will connect you to your local center. Within a couple of days, someone will come to your home and mark your utilities for free. For more information, visit www.call811.com.

TOP LEFT Use a pergola or other type of structure as a focal point that gives your garden a destination. This vine-draped pergola (walled in by an "L" of arborvitae evergreens) sits at the end of a path that winds through tall plants, including carefree roses, phlox, and sunflowers.

LEFT Pull a garden room away from the back of the house for a different point of view. This simple pavilion offers a comfortable vantage point along the back fence and overlooks a small but sparkly cool pool.

Let your personal style determine the path your outdoor room takes. A weathered pergola and a vintage dining set mark this room as country. The vines link to other naturalized plantings.

ABOVE Design with an abundance of the same plant—or flowering plants of the same color—for a calm, monochromatic outdoor scheme. Natural wicker and lush layers of hydrangea, broken up only by rich foliage, weave together in a sophisticated manner.

ABOVE The best garden spaces are often the simplest ones. A floor of flagstone and a bistro table make this an outdoor room. Planting beds between the flagstone and wood fence soften those hard elements. The mix of ornamental trees, flowering shrubs, and mounding perennials keeps the beds low maintenance.

backyard trees and shrubs

● ● ● A BOWER OF TREES IN YOUR BACKYARD provides some pretty dandy benefits. The most obvious are cooling shade, fruits and nuts (for us and our animal friends), and shelter for all kinds of wildlife. The roots prevent erosion and filter out pollutants. The leaves filter airborne pollutants and store carbon dioxide, which helps counter greenhouse gases. For you, trees will increase your property value and improve the aesthetics of your home. To see the most benefit, know your soil type and USDA Plant Hardiness Zones (see the map on p. 180) to plant trees and shrubs that will grow happily without a lot of special care. And be sure to leave plenty of room for that growth: The most common mistake home gardeners make is planting trees too close together or too snug to structures.

Low-growing shrubs offer interest at eye level, filling in dark corners or bridging the gap between trees and turf. Depending on the growing habit, shrubs can line up into a tidy privacy hedge or add airy elegance to a garden bed. Though shrubs were once mostly relegated to lining a house's foundation like a frilly hem, today, shrubs help define areas within a backyard's boundaries and add beauty throughout the landscape.

Some hardwood trees grow faster than others, an important quality for new construction. Pin and bur oaks are two varieties that will grow to the roofline within a few years.

LEFT Hardwood trees don't grow as fast as softwood varieties, but they make up for their slow and steady growth by living much longer. Hardwoods such as oak, walnut, or hickory trees can be pruned to allow light to reach undergrowth, as evident at this Texas home.

ABOVE Plant shrubs in a raised bed to give them a boost in height for more privacy. This mixed hedge is planted two and three plants deep in a bed held in place by an artful poured-cement edge.

LEFT Mature hardwood trees add value to a property. This Iowa homeowner left part of her small acreage natural, letting the tall oaks that shade her house and dot her field blend together a manicured lawn and free-growing meadow.

planting the backyard 77

•the best backyard trees

Trees are the plantings that will essentially create the framework of your backyard—now and for decades to come. Shop carefully, paying particular attention to indigenous varieties that require less maintenance, are resistant to disease and infestation, and will grow sturdy and strong for years or even decades.

Plant a variety of trees and you'll have a more vibrant landscape, one that serves up color and interest through the seasons. Review these charts for some top trees based on vitality, landscape flexibility, and popularity.

top tall-growing trees

Tall, slow-growing deciduous trees offer a good return on your investment—if you're patient. Though they only grow inches per year, their wood is dense and strong, making them stand up to rough weather and other dangers.

VARIETY	ZONES	DESCRIPTION
Red maple	Zones 3–9	This tree has it all. It is hardy through all zones in the United States and Canada, growing to about 40 to 70 feet tall in a relatively short time. You'll enjoy its scarlet red color in the fall. There are many hardy maples, but avoid the silver maple, which is shorter lived and requires regular pruning to stay healthy.
Yellow poplar (aka "Tulip tree")	Zones 3–9	With its tidy columnar growing habit and yellow-orange, tulip-like blossoms in the spring, the yellow poplar is popular throughout the United States, through Zone 5. This fast grower will reach 70 to 90 feet tall, but will offer you a nice pool of shade within a couple of years.
Oak	Zones 3–9	There are native oak species across the country—which is why the Arbor Day Foundation named the mighty oak this country's first national tree. From the romantic live oaks of the South to the gigantic red and white oaks of the heartland to the blue oaks of California, there is an oak variety just right for your area. Pin and bur oaks will gain height more quickly than other oak varieties.
American sycamore	Zones 4–9	The sycamore tree is one of the easiest (and fastest!) of the big trees to grow thanks to its tolerance of most any soil conditions. And grow it will, reaching over 100 feet high at maturity. Though the tree can be messy, with shedding bark and seed pods to keep after, its creamy bark and massive, broadleaf stature make it an ever-popular backyard tree.
Hickory	Zones 4–8	Shagbark hickory trees are indigenous to the United States and loved for their intriguing, peeling bark and golden autumn leaves. Another one of the tall-tree varieties, this tough tree can reach a height of 130 feet.

best small trees

Small and flowering trees fill in your landscape with color and texture to add softness and dimension to a small yard. These are understory species—trees that mature to about 30 feet tall or less, that naturally grow beneath the big trees of the forest and are used to less light.

VARIETY	ZONES	DESCRIPTION
Crabapple	Zones 4–9	There's a reason why many varieties of crabapples grace yards across North America. They brighten spring with small pompom blossoms that pop out in shades of orange, gold, and pink on character-rich, often gnarly structure. You can pick your favorite growth habit, too. There are types with weeping, columnar, or lollipop-round growing patterns that reach a range of 6 feet for dwarf varieties to 30 feet for standard varieties.
Dogwood	Zones 4–8	With an appealing, airy branch pattern, this popular understory tree announces spring with showy pink or white blossoms, then finishes the season with deep red foliage and berries. Though a mainstay of the southern landscape, Northerners can look for native varieties such as 'Cherokee Chief' or 'Cherokee Sunset' that thrive from Zones 5 to 8 or 'Pagoda' dogwoods that grow through Zone 4.
Serviceberry	Zones 5–8	If you want a petite tree that serves up a bonus each season, take a look at one of the 20 varieties of serviceberry trees. White blooms in spring give way to purple or red berries in the summer that will draw birds (or harvest the edible varieties to make jam!). Fiery red foliage in the fall drops to reveal silver bark.
Redbud	Zones 5–9	This small ornamental tree features dark, slender limbs that reach to 30 feet wide. In the spring, the limbs are dotted with vivid purple-pink or white blooms. A native to the eastern United States, this tree prefers sun.
Hawthorn	Zones 4–7	The puffy white flowers of the hawthorn tree don't show up until June, but its large red berries last well into winter and are a favorite snack of songbirds. Autumn color adds another layer of interest for this compact tree.

easy-growing evergreens

Evergreen trees lend year-round structure and interest to backyard landscapes. These tree varieties naturally conserve moisture and nutrients, making them easy to grow in many conditions.

VARIETY	ZONES	DESCRIPTION
Eastern white pine	Zones 3–8	This tree's long, soft needles easily move on the breeze, making it a graceful counterpart to its stiff and often bristly conifer cousins. Use this indigenous tree to attract wildlife, offer a wind buffer, or just to add year-round beauty to your yard.
Blue spruce	Zones 3–8	Add blue-gray hue to your backyard with this evergreen, which can grow up to 50 feet. There are a number of varieties of blue spruce, including those that grow in a columnar shape.
Eastern red cedar	Zones 2–9	Also known as Virginia juniper, this drought-resistant conifer is one of the most widely distributed trees in North America, native to 37 states. It's loved for its blue berries in winter and fragrant bark.
Frasier fir	Zones 3–7	The Frasier fir, and its close cousin the Balsam fir, present the perfect Christmas tree shape—which is why they are classic favorites to bring inside for the holiday. In your landscape, they serve up the same woodsy scent, pyramidal shape, and deep green leaves. Firs will grow up to 60 feet at the pace of 1 to 2 feet per year, making the sturdy trees popular in wind breaks.
Canadian hemlock	Zones 3–7	This native to the East Coast features small needles that give it a fine, feathery appearance, especially in the chartreuse new growth. This slow-growing evergreen can reach over 80 feet tall, though some compact varieties can also be used as hedgerow. The shallow roots on this conifer make it susceptible to wind damage, so it's best planted in a protected area. The good news is it doesn't mind a bit of shade.

• hedges

Fences preserve backyard privacy and keep pets on the property. But sometimes they just don't match the fluid, natural environment you want for your home environs. A living wall created by densely planted shrubs or flowering bushes might be your answer. Planted in a row and often pruned to perfection, a classic hedge is dense enough to enclose your space, screen a view (or screen your family from view), and keep your surroundings soft. Just remember, living walls demand more time and energy than a static fence line.

Hedgerows are an investment, so it pays to pick your plants wisely. For a precise, homogenous hedge, evergreens might be your best bet. For a looser lineup that offers fragrance to boot, bring home a series of blooming honeysuckle. Or layer a mix of evergreen and deciduous shrubs for more texture and dimension. Think about how your plants might entertain you through the seasons or attract wildlife to your own little world. Blackhaw viburnum, for instance, will share its white blossoms in the spring, pretty berries in the summer, and burnished leaves in the fall.

Hedges don't need to be limited to the perimeter of a yard. In this formal landscape, a row of boxwood is trimmed into a geometric pattern like a partial wall to divide the eating area from the pool.

ABOVE Marry a hedgerow with a privacy fence for a backyard perimeter that has dimension, texture, and a natural look. Here, evergreens with an upright growth pattern are interspersed with a low-growing variety for a full look.

ABOVE Fast-growing deciduous shrubs with an upright growth habit will become a private enclosure within a couple of years. Perfect for narrow spaces, the buckthorn hedge has a uniform appearance that works well with modern settings.

more hedge ideas

For more fullness and privacy, don't limit your perimeter plantings to one type of plant. Underplant "leggy" shrubs with a skirt of dwarf English boxwoods for a lush living wall.

ABOVE By definition, a hedge is plants, shrubs, or trees planted close together to form a boundary. So be creative! A row of non-invasive, clumping bamboo softens a fence line in this outdoor living room, but it is used to filter a view, too.

FAR LEFT Southwestern dwellers have their own idea of easy-care hedge plantings. The deciduous ocotillo plant becomes modern art when tucked into a raised cement bed.

LEFT Trained to climb over arbors, crawl along fences, or stand alone as bushes, roses create romantic and fragrant perimeter plantings. When planted close together, roses can become quite tight-knit, in effect, forming a hedge, as evidenced in this California backyard, where the arbors of roses give this landscape more intimacy and a sense a discovery.

fences

● ● ● FENCES MAKE CLASSIC PARTNERS FOR plantings, adding a uniform, structural backdrop to contrast with freewheeling plant life. Some fences make prime multitaskers, lending privacy, protection, and pet containment while they mark out the perimeter of your property. Decide what functions you need a fence for, then shop for an option that complements your architecture and landscaping style. Consider all of the material choices as well. Here's how a few common materials stack up:

- **Chain-link** fence is the least expensive and most long-lasting fencing option. Though more utilitarian in style, chain-link fences can be screened with plantings or woven with vinyl tape to improve their look and privacy factor.

- **Wood** will eat more deeply into your budget, but the way wood's natural good looks blend with the natural environment makes the payoff worth it for some. You can choose from different heights and materials to help wood fit more easily into the budget.

- **Vinyl** fencing is significantly more expensive than wood, but it is virtually maintenance-free and stands up over time (though don't count on vinyl panels to resist the weight of a big dog without snapping). Less expensive plastic or composite fencing will save you dollars but will not hold up like the stronger vinyl over time.

- **Wrought iron** fences are a handsome finishing touch for the yard. But this classic material is also the most expensive. To save money, look for premade panels found in home improvement stores.

Layer fences to create the multidimensional effect of full and partial walls like those inside the house. A wood privacy fence keeps the backyard pool private, while the rail fence with its wire mesh screen adds an extra layer of security and structure.

ABOVE Twist your thinking cap a little to invent new ways for using familiar materials. Fencing installed horizontally and stained becomes intriguing modern paneling.

TOP RIGHT Cut cinderblock creates a filigreed border that is part fence and part wall. Tap into your creativity next time you're at the home improvement store, where building materials abound.

BOTTOM RIGHT Wrought iron fences are a classic choice that weave together easily with most design styles. Use vintage fences as decorative items within the garden, or make a statement by selecting a modern iron fence for your perimeter.

walls

● ● ● OUTDOOR WALLS ARE PART OF THE beautiful bones of your garden. But they also serve practical purposes. Retaining walls of stone or wood can be designed to hold back thousands of pounds of earth or turn a sloping or unstable terrain into a more usable flat plane. Freestanding walls aren't used to hold back elevations, but do add to the function and charm of your space. Freestanding walls can outline garden rooms, support built-in benches, or create a focal point. And walls of all sorts make perfect companions to plants and vines.

Before you grab your shovel, check the building codes in your community. Many codes require a permit for walls over 3 feet high. Regardless, it's a good idea to work with a landscape designer or contractor if you are considering wall construction. Landscape walls need to be engineered to drain water away from the wall (and often your foundation) and direct it to an optimal route.

Concrete can be cast into endless shapes, sizes, and uses. This low-slung wall serves as a bench and fire surround while creating a visual enclosure for a seating area.

ABOVE Left bare or planted with flowers, retaining walls make pretty—and practical—perimeters for outdoor rooms, since they also can double as seating. This mortared stone is a backdrop for a perennial bed on one side and a back to a built-in bench on the other.

LEFT Low walls are a great addition to a patio. Not only do they help enclose the space, providing intimacy, but they allow for extra seating when having a casual gathering.

more about...
CHOOSING WALL MATERIALS

t he materials you pick for your outdoor wall should reflect the style of your home and garden and be strong enough to do the job.

• **Natural stone.** Though it can be expensive, stone is also permanent. For a natural look, it can't be beat. To keep costs down, shop for local stone.

• **Manufactured stone.** This engineered material has made leaps forward in both style and strength. Concrete blocks and pavers come in all hues and textures, and are harder than building bricks. Better yet, they are less expensive than stone or building brick and are easier to install.

• **Poured concrete.** For a clean, modern style, many homeowners are turning to the smooth good looks of poured concrete. The material is successfully used in mild climates, where cracking isn't an issue. Tricky to engineer, this type of divider is best left to concrete contractors.

• **Wood.** Wood blends into the natural environment as readily as stone. Though not as long-lasting as stone, walls created of pressure-treated woods will hold up for many years if water is not allowed to pool on or behind the wood structure. Look for wood that is marked suitable for ground contact.

beds and borders

●●● THERE IS AN ALTERNATIVE TO CONSTRUCTING walls and digging fence posts: You can grow your own privacy screens and garden "walls" with perennial flowers and foliage. To pick the right plants for the job, first you need to do a background check of sorts. Check labels, growers' tips, or your favorite botanical resources for a plant's needs and growing habits to determine if the plant will be happy where you put it and, likewise, if you will be happy with it.

Books and plant labels will give you the average height and width of a plant as part of its growth habit, which will help you figure location and spacing. The trick for most gardeners is to create a full effect as soon as possible, without causing unhealthy (and unruly!) overcrowding a couple of years down the line. One way to keep your bed balanced is to pick plants with varying bloom times. When spring flowers fade out, summer bloomers kick in and so on through the seasons. For the best effect, select two or three plants from each growing season. Sprinkle in evergreens, ornamental trees, or grasses for structure.

Watch out for one word on a plant's description before you work it into your backyard plan—vigor. Vigor can be a good thing, indicating that a plant will spread, drift, and cover more territory for a good return on your investment. But a "vigorous grower" could also mean an aggressive plant that can crowd out other plants and take over your garden. Any gardener will tell you that rearranging—and rethinking—planting schemes to better match plant with a plot is part of developing a property.

Easy-growing ornamental grasses are cropping up in all types of beds and borders. To soften the foreground of this treetop view and add a layer of privacy on their deck, these owners used raised beds filled with softly swaying variegated grasses.

A retaining wall and raised garden bed will lift your planted border for a pretty and private combination. A natural rock wall lets flowers tumble over its façade for a lush layered look.

• types of beds and borders

Whether you look out on a flat, sloping, oddly shaped, large, or teensy-weensy yard, there are just a few types of flowerbeds to consider that will match a variety of landscape scenarios.

There are two basic types of garden beds: The border and the island. A border garden is usually designed to be viewed from one side and is accompanied by some type of vertical backdrop. Typically, this bed is a long, rectangular-shaped patch that is 2 to 4 feet deep and 10 to 15 feet long. Just remember not to dig up more than you can keep up! Allow space or plan a small footpath within the garden so you can tend to individual plants and allow a bit of negative space to define each one.

An island bed, as its name suggests, is designed to float within a sea of turf or other type of ground covering. In this type of arrangement, tall plants are placed in the middle and low-growers are located around the outside of a mounded bed, or landscape berm. Stagger plant heights within the two extremes. The shape of your private island is up to you, but keep proportions in mind. Generously sized islands—at least 8 feet by 15 feet with a 5-foot rise— are the most visually appealing.

Don't feel penned in by these borders. Rock or shade gardens often take the shape of the terrain or shade lines for a naturalized approach. Or consider a combination of the border and island bed and create a corner garden to soften the edges of your yard.

Deep beds of bloom can soften a foundation and knit a house to its landscape with color and texture. This lush, 6-foot-deep bed blooms throughout the seasons and uses grasses for height and structure.

A mix of evergreens, blooming shrubs, and trees creates an inviting mix of structure and softness. A plush runner of turf cuts a path between this border and island bed.

Flowerbeds don't have to be large to command attention. The banana plant creates the perfect backdrop for daisies and mums.

specialty gardens

● ● ● CREATIVE GARDENERS AND LANDSCAPE experts are constantly expanding the boundaries of what a private outdoor haven can entail. Would you like to read by your own gurgling stream? Grow food with your flowers? Create a landscape that demands little in terms of your time and resources? Go for it. The limits of your yard matter less than those you place on your own imagination.

Or take cues from your site and familiar types of specialty gardens to create your own spin on the classics. Shade gardens, succulent beds, woodland wildflower schemes—there are many creative ways to work within the lay of your land and the bounds of your budget and personal taste to create your own garden expression.

Water is a soothing feature in the landscape and feels more natural when surrounded by plantings. Many water plants, like these grasses, are hardy, so can thrive in shade or partial sun. Low-growing evergreens and some perennials are other natural choices.

ABOVE Succulents and cactus provide enough variety to soften even the starkest desert garden. This raised-bed garden features an artful mix of Southwestern plantings set against a cool white wall for eye-catching contrast.

LEFT Plants and stones are a natural border combination, and one that can be easy to care for. This patio edge stays casual with a loose collection of stacked stones interplanted with the drought-resistant plant silver mound that will fill in like mortar to stabilize the rocks.

• edible landscaping

The trend in edible landscaping is now a full-grown movement, having taken root all across the country as a part of the "Buy Fresh, Buy Local" campaign. Food really can't get fresher or more local than the type you grow out your own back door. But don't think you need to sow row crops or give up flowers to add some edible plants into your overall landscaping.

Simply defined, edible landscaping is the integration of food plants with ornamental plants in a decorative setting. Think frilly spring green lettuces, cute blueberry bushes, or bright rhubarb woven among your favorite flowers and you can quickly get the picture. An edible garden is a way to blend utility with pure beauty and make your backyard more productive.

Think of a backyard vegetable garden as a decorative element and you can plant one anywhere. Natural pine lumber assembles into a raised, nontoxic garden bed that softens a simple California courtyard.

ABOVE Flowering herbs and vegetables with frilly foliage look as pretty as any perennial plant, so why not grow them together. This formal, raised-bed garden includes blooming sage and rhubarb, plus many flowering specimens.

SOIL HEALTH AND WOOD PRESERVATIVES

t he concern about preservatives and other potentially toxic materials leaching from pressure-treated woods and recycled railroad ties into surrounding soil has us rethinking edible garden materials. Switch to foundation-grade redwood or cedar, which is a more expensive but healthy choice, when constructing raised beds and retaining walls of wood.

ABOVE Garden beds look more unified if they are planted with a cohesive palette in mind. Eggplants and purple coleus create design rhythm in this terraced border garden.

• ponds and creeks

The marriage of stone, water, and plant life is a beautiful thing. Backyard ponds, streams, and waterfalls deliver the sights and sounds of the natural world to your backyard, along with all the relaxation benefits of a trip to the countryside. Visually, glistening streambeds and basins of water are eye-grabbers, especially when combined with plant life. Often they're problem solvers too. A sloping yard is a natural for a manufactured creek. A flat terrain could gain interest from a small pond and a casual border of boulders.

Although anything is possible, remember that the more earth you need to move to realize your water wonderland will mean more cash outlay. Work with your site's individual characteristics to make the most out of your resources.

FACING PAGE FAR LEFT Water gardening opens up a whole new world of plant life. You don't need a large body of water to experiment with colorful water plants such as this water lily.

FACING PAGE LEFT A naturally flowing creek bed can spring up wherever there is a rise in your yard. This manufactured brook starts in a side yard, where natural boulders and swaying grasses hide its true origins.

TOP RIGHT Surround a pond with stones and grasses to prevent soil erosion into the water. This small pond includes a waterfall for its calming sound. Plus, the movement keeps the water cleaner.

BOTTOM RIGHT If your landscape includes a slope, make the most of it. This backyard scheme takes advantage of a dramatically rising terrain to create a natural-looking but totally manufactured creek bed.

entertaining out back

• • •

WITH NATURE AS YOUR CO-HOST, AN OUTDOOR SETTING DOESN'T need to be elaborate to be memorable. Still, there are some essentials that will make your backyard events easier to enjoy, for both you and your guests.

To start, keep in mind that entertaining in the open air is not unlike relaxing indoors. You'll need easy access to your party zone, comfortable places to sit, and a way to control the temperature. Throw in some pretty things to look at and some practical ways to stay organized (and more relaxed!) when hosting parties or everyday family gatherings. Easy cleanup and storage when entertaining help to keep the event running smoothly.

Before you plan your outdoor entertaining area, think about your style. Do you like to host formal dinner parties to show off your culinary skills? Or do you prefer a laid-back cookout where comfort is key? Do your parties tend to transition into nighttime hours where lighting would be necessary for mood and safety?

Furniture and fabrics have improved in both style and substance, adding a final layer of comfort and color to outdoor settings. This covered deck is cleverly designed to look like a part of the pool with the extended cement border. The pergola protects outdoor furniture and fabrics from sun and rain.

Maybe you like intimate cocktail parties where conversation flows easily and cozy privacy rules. Think about the most enjoyable parties you've been to or the most successful parties you've thrown to come up with a list of attributes for your backyard gathering spot. This chapter will open your eyes to the many options available to you.

the outdoor kitchen

● ● ● NOT SO LONG AGO, COOKING OUT MEANT nothing more than a grill and a bag of charcoal. Now, an outdoor kitchen can be as elaborate as an upscale restaurant kitchen, complete with stone pizza oven and wine fridge. But it doesn't have to be. Plan an outdoor cook space to suit your site, style, and budget, starting with the basics.

A good grill is the centerpiece of an outdoor kitchen. For most outdoor chefs, a 35-inch grill has enough surface area to handle family meals and parties. Many gas grills now have attached prep surfaces, but most aren't much larger than a dinner plate. Consider whether you want your grill to be built into a countertop or freestanding, with a roll-up island or prep surface at the ready. Most landscape architects suggest at least 12 inches of surface space on either side of the grill. But more is more in this case, especially if you like to socialize while you cook. Add extra counter surface and pull up a couple of stools for a multi-tasking prep surface, serving area, and additional dining space.

No matter the size, select durable surfaces that are suited to your climate. Stainless steel, stone, slate, or tile are the most common choices, but whatever you choose, make certain the material is designed for exterior use. Tile is an affordable choice, but be sure to finish it with latex grout that expands and contracts with weather changes.

LEFT An outdoor kitchen doesn't have to be built in to be functional. Here, the color palette of the space makes the stainless steel grill feel more connected thanks to galvanized fencing, warm woods, and mesh seating.

ABOVE Build in prep surfaces on either side of a built-in grill to make cooking and serving easier. This table is pulled near the grill for ease and to keep the cook close to the action.

FACING PAGE Use decking materials creatively to create an outdoor kitchen that extends a home's indoor style. Teak boards clad an island in this modern setting. The island holds a sink and needed storage.

LEFT Design an outdoor kitchen with ample storage and surfaces that pull double duty. Natural wood and stone create open and closed storage in this efficient, compact kitchen. A counter serves as a bar and casual dining spot.

•outdoor kitchen amenities

An outdoor kitchen doesn't have to be large or elaborate. Here are a few features that will add to the comfort and efficiency of an outdoor cooking area. Stack them up against your budget to see which ones would be a worthwhile investment for your family.

- Multiple **power outlets** will allow you to bring small appliances, such as blenders or food warmers, and portable electronics to your outdoor dining.

- An **outdoor sink** can be tied to a house's existing plumbing lines or simply fed from a garden hose. In cold climates, special care will need to be taken to insulate the lines or clear them if freezing is an issue.

- A **refrigerator** can be built in or left freestanding. The most important thing is to find one suitable for outdoor use. These typically compact units are designed to be safe in wet conditions, resist rusting, and better handle fluctuating outdoor temperatures.

- **Electronics** can be the life of any outdoor party. If audio or video equipment is a permanent part of your plan, look for those especially designed to be waterproof and weatherproof unless they are going to be well-protected from the elements, such as in an enclosed pavilion or porch.

Include extra counter and storage space to add more function and convenience to a simple outdoor kitchen. Next to this built-in grill, a small cooktop and refrigerator bring the convenience of a full kitchen outdoors.

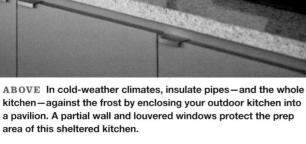

ABOVE In cold-weather climates, insulate pipes—and the whole kitchen—against the frost by enclosing your outdoor kitchen into a pavilion. A partial wall and louvered windows protect the prep area of this sheltered kitchen.

TOP RIGHT Whether used for cleaning vegetables from the garden or rinsing out the barware, an outdoor sink can save you many steps back and forth from inside the house. This small stainless type is built into a granite countertop and links to the home's plumbing.

BOTTOM RIGHT Outdoor refrigerators can be freestanding or built in and are typically smaller than indoor types. This built-in unit is vented out the front and features a lock for safety.

•outdoor kitchen storage

Planning for the storage components of an outdoor kitchen is as important as designing an indoor cooking zone. Along with picking the right grill and counter space, think about storage and organizational extras for items you'll want to keep close at hand. The good news is that backyard kitchens aren't as demanding as their indoor counterparts—you need the goods for just one meal rather than a week's menu.

A protected cupboard, built-in niches, or an inexpensive exterior storage cart can stash dinnerware, grill utensils, and cleaning gear. Consider real helpers such as pullout trash and recycling bins.

One note of caution, though, if you are adding an elaborate outdoor kitchen to an existing deck—make sure there is enough support to hold the extra weight. Check local codes to see if a permit is required for this type of construction. Local zoning laws also address outdoor electrical issues and fire safety codes.

Stainless steel is a sleek, rustproof material to use in the elements. This stainless-clad counter joins poured cement for a tidy but efficient cooking center that includes an ice well for entertaining.

more
about...
OUTDOOR KITCHEN EXTRAS

• **An outdoor ceiling fan** helps circulate the air, especially in a semi-closed space.

• **Built-in, UL-rated "wet" lighting** will extend the hours you can cook and serve outdoors.

• **A small kitchen garden** or a few pots of favorite herbs near the grill will keep fresh ingredients nearby.

• **A partial roof** or awning will keep the cook and his or her companions dry and shaded.

LEFT Keep components light and efficient when creating an outdoor kitchen on a raised wood deck. A stainless grill and storage components are tucked into a painted wood counter and storage well.

RIGHT Borrow elements from architecture for seamless outdoor kitchen style. A stone buffet topped with honed granite will last for decades, making the initial investment worthwhile. Multiple niches were created to slide in outdoor appliances and storage.

furniture for outdoor dining

● ● ● COMFORTABLE, GOOD-LOOKING, AND LONG-wearing furniture makes an impact on how you enjoy your alfresco dining area, so it pays to shop wisely. Though the sheer number of choices in styles and materials on the market can be daunting, your choice really boils down to four basic types: wood, metal, wicker, and resins.

Wood furniture sets a casual, natural mood. Pine and cedar, the most commonly used woods, will weather to a silvery gray unless you seal them against the elements. Cedar is typically pricier than pressure-treated pine, but both types can last for years. Teak is the costliest of wood options, but this tropical hardwood will last for 50 years. Look for newer options, such as Ipê, a tropical hardwood. Be sure tropical woods carry the Forest Stewardship Council certification to ensure they've been sustainably harvested.

Metal is probably the most popular type of outdoor furniture thanks to its toughness and versatility; plus it's offered at all price points. The most common metals you'll find are wrought iron and aluminum. Wrought iron takes a traditional style bent, while aluminum tends to be extruded into clean, modern expressions.

Wicker conjures up romance and classic cottage style. Shop for all-weather wicker for seating that will hold up to the elements—just hose it off when dirty. Natural wicker should be used in covered outdoor areas only, where the fibers aren't exposed to moisture.

Resin furniture, essentially molded plastic, is a budget-lover's choice for outdoor seating or lounging. It's also easy to clean and portable. For an upgrade in both style and quality, shop for designer resin pieces, which are sleek, boldly colored patio fare. Marine-grade polymers or recycled plastics are sturdy choices.

Recycled materials in both wood and plastic outdoor furnishings are an option for ecologically conscious home-owners. This pallet wood makes a clever dining table that's been given casters for easy moving.

LEFT Modern seating and comfortable extras like ceiling fans and a roof combine into an inviting alfresco setting in rain or warm sunshine. Molded into organic shapes, resin dining chairs add a pop of color to the patio of this ranch house.

ABOVE Metals such as wrought iron and aluminum have long been used on traditional outdoor furniture. These graceful aluminum pieces are lightweight for easy lifting. Cushions will keep you comfortable when sitting for long periods of time.

LEFT Simple, slatted teak wood is a classic choice for outdoor dining furniture. Even unfinished, teak furniture lasts for decades, fading to a silvery gray as it ages.

gallery

outdoor dining furniture

RIGHT Mix furniture styles and add fresh pops of color to create a more personal and inviting dining area. Modern lightweight aluminum chairs in a classic slat-back design coordinate with a turned farmhouse table and buffet that have been given a protective coat of pool-blue outdoor paint.

BELOW Resist the urge to buy suites of matching furniture, or your backyard living spaces might have all the charm and personality of a furniture store. Instead, buy well-designed pieces that blend easily together. Honey-toned dining furniture is neutral enough to sit comfortably next to simply designed armchairs in earth-toned outdoor fabrics.

LEFT Add fresh pops of color to create a more personal and inviting outdoor living area. Outdoor cushions with geranium-red accents plump up modern lightweight aluminum chairs in a classic sling-back design, offering a sleek-lined contrast to a traditional house.

ABOVE You don't need a patio or deck to carve out an alfresco spot for casual dining and entertaining. Thanks to its large scale, sturdy and stocky teak furniture gives a sense of enclosure, especially when topped with a large umbrella standing in for a roof.

LEFT Opt for a covered back deck or porch and you'll uncover more options in dining furniture. Thanks to its location next to the woodstove, this vintage cottage furniture serves outside for three seasons until it's stored for the winter.

the backyard living room

● ● ● A PATIO, DECK, OR GRASSY BACKYARD corner provides a ready perimeter for a relaxing outdoor living room, but the decorating options have no boundaries. Narrow your choices by thinking about how you will most likely use your outdoor relaxation zone. Outdoor seating pieces can take the shape of tucked-in benches or fully cushioned sofas. Vary the type and height of seating and their companion tables for a more dynamic scheme and to expand your entertaining options. Just don't throw in so many that traffic patterns become cluttered.

The most successful outdoor room designs, like their adjacent indoor schemes, start with a focal point piece that is large enough or interesting enough to grab the eye first. Start there, then group your pieces in cozy arrangements divided by activity. Use outdoor rugs to anchor secondary groupings and add tall container plantings as screening between the groupings. Mostly, remember that the best part of decorating an outdoor room is that it's all about fun and relaxation.

Synthetic wicker can be shaped into classic cottage or sleek modern shapes, and it holds up better to the weather than the old paper types of wicker.

ABOVE Think about flexibility of furniture arrangements. Lightweight wicker pieces can be pulled close for conversation or moved in front of a fireplace on a chilly night.

more about...
OUTDOOR FURNITURE MATERIALS

omfort and good looks are just part of the outdoor decorating equation. Furnishings for outdoor rooms need to hold up to nature's extremes and the everyday wear and tear of life in the sun and rain.

• **Metal** pieces should boast powder-coated, UV-protected finishes that are baked into the material at the manufacturing stage.

• **Plastic or resin** furnishings should be made of UV-stabilizing pigments so they won't lose their colors in the sun.

• **Wood** pieces should feature screwed construction rather than glued. Look for steel screws that won't rust.

LEFT New hardwoods, such as ipê from Central and South America, are harder and longer lasting than teak. Ipê has a dark finish that resembles walnut, perfect for this traditional seating area.

• outdoor fabrics

Advances in textile manufacturing have done a lot to boost the color and comfort of backyards everywhere. For the most part, you can thank solution-dyed acrylic fabrics, where color is added at the fiber stage before it is converted to yarn and woven into a fabric. The resulting fabric is soft, comfortable, and breathable even while it resists sun fading and water—and it does all this while managing to feel like cotton. Sunbrella® is the best-known name in solution-dyed acrylics. Once concerned with only boats and awnings, this company is credited with ushering in pretty patterns and colors when it turned to residential outdoor fabrics.

A new name in backyard fabrics is one you may not recognize, but you're likely familiar with its products: Crypton® Super Fabrics. These polyester fabrics had previously been available only to hospitals, restaurants, and hotels. What makes them super? A moisture barrier and disinfectant agents that are baked into every fiber, making the resulting fabric virtually waterproof—and stain- and bacteria-resistant to boot. Like the acrylics, the Crypton fabrics come in decorator widths (54 inches) for those who are can sew their own cushions.

FACING PAGE New advances in outdoor fabric means there's no need to worry about cleaning and upkeep of cushions and curtains. Though these home-owners know to extend the life of fabrics by bringing cushions indoors when possible, they aren't afraid of white outdoor fabrics thanks to new easy-clean properties.

RIGHT Both printed and woven outdoor fabrics are available in rich hues and bold patterns. This patio set becomes a focal point when the tiered umbrella is opened; the umbrella fabric also ties together the outdoor color scheme, from the orange cushions to the tree roses.

BELOW Crisply colored non-fade fabrics will stay bright thanks to the color baked into the fibers. This pool house takes advantage of the softening power of fabrics on curtains, cushions, pillows, and umbrellas.

Printed acrylics and printed polyester outdoor fabrics are less expensive than the solution-dyed acrylics and new polyesters (which both run over $30 per yard) and are widely available. These soft but durable textiles dry quickly and resist fading but don't have the UV protection that the solution-dyed acrylics offer. Olefin is considered the toughest wearing of these synthetics, but fabric woven of olefin lacks the softness and easy draping of acrylic.

Finally, PVC mesh or vinyl-coated synthetic fiber mesh (most commonly known as "sling" fabrics) are designed to support a sitting person, so you know they're tough. As such, they can be scrubbed, hosed off, bleached, and left in sun and rain with no fading or mildew issues. These textiles aren't as soft as the others, but they're more colorful than ever.

Today's ready-made cushions are built to last, covered in fade-proof fabrics. For extended-wear cushions, make sure the filler is also formulated to handle rain or moisture as is the case with these box cushions and chaise pads.

BELOW Outdoor fabrics become more beautiful, available, and affordable each year. And they aren't just for cushions and pillows. Re-create a backyard space with fabric that moves with the breeze while adding privacy and shade.

ABOVE Outfit a simple bench with plump cushions and pillows for a clever outdoor sectional.

more about...
CARING FOR OUTDOOR FABRICS

Outdoor fabrics are primarily synthetics. Though they differ in composition, they have commonalities in care.

- **Do not dry clean.** Brush dirt and debris from pillows and cushions regularly. These synthetics can be spot-cleaned and freshened with a solution of ¼ cup of bleach-free detergent in 1 gallon of warm water.

- **Do not tumble dry**—and you shouldn't have to since the textiles are all quick to dry.

- **Although the fabric is water resistant**, it isn't waterproof. Get to spills quickly while they are pooling and remember to bring in cushions when rain is in the forecast.

- **Outdoor fabrics do not promote** mildew and mold growth, though spills and sitting liquids can grow this nastiness. Be sure fabrics are allowed to dry completely after liquid exposure.

- **All outdoor textiles**—from awnings to cushion covers—are UV rated by the manufacturer, which indicates hours of sunshine they will endure before fading. Most woven acrylics are rated for 1,500 light hours or more. Printed or woven polyesters and printed acrylics are rated for 500 to 750 hours of rays.

LEFT A small pond pump and a large, water-worthy vessel is the easiest way to add the soothing sound of water to your outdoor living areas. Terra-cotta is a natural accent to bring to the garden, but fill a clay pot with water instead of plant life for a new twist.

BELOW Although portable electronics are the norm, consider all your options when thinking about music. This speaker is weatherproof and readily blends into the landscape.

ABOVE Put more fun in your surroundings with outdoor art designed to surprise and bring a smile. This wooden cow cutout peeks out from a naturalized meadow that borders this in-town acreage.

LEFT Fill in stark areas of the garden with naturalized art. These metal flowers bridge a visual gap between low-growing plants and a high fence. The artwork offers pops of color and moves in the breeze to attract birds and butterflies.

backyard structures

• • •

A SECONDARY STRUCTURE DRAMATICALLY CHANGES THE way your backyard looks and lives. From simple pergolas to modern dining pavilions, a small structure brings dimension and height to a landscape, plus a fabulous focal point to build your terrain around.

The visual aspect is just one bonus of a secondary building—there's also the fun and functional side of backyard structures. There are so many types of kits, plans, and ready-made buildings on the market, that you're limited only by your lot lines, local building codes, and imagination.

For instance, you can order a cool chicken coop kit, sized for a city lot and delivered to your back door. Need a little getaway to indulge your creative side? Order up building plans for an architect-designed personal art studio, garden house, or any type of backyard room. There are cute sheds to hold your kids' toys—or your lawn toys. This chapter will explore a variety of options for bringing more design and livability to your landscape.

Designers and homeowners are finding creative solutions to outdoor living spaces. By pulling this screened structure away from the house and making it easily accessed by a covered walkway, the owners created a dramatic dining pavilion with a view.

garden rooms

• • • Structures related to the garden are natural extensions of a backyard layered with plant life. Outbuildings that take their design cues from your home's architecture will add personal style as well as a beautiful backdrop for plants. Or open up the structure for a place to enjoy a shade break and entertain friends while admiring your landscape. It's all about you. Create an inspiring space suited to your interests, and you'll find yourself enjoying the outdoors much more often.

Poolside pavilions offer shade and an intimate spot for alfresco dining. Panels of outdoor fabric block out UV rays and pump up the romance in this classic, lattice-walled pavilion.

ABOVE A garden room doesn't have to be a permanent structure. This tent stays up for the season, offering a shady place to enjoy the setting. Side curtains add privacy and softness.

RIGHT Garden houses are a chance to make the most of your property and extend your living space in a personal way. As its carved door and moon announce, this rustic country getaway tucked into the woods is a peaceful guest house and meditation room.

•potting and puttering sheds

Most of us need some sort of structure to function as storage and workspace for our backyard gardening endeavors. Before you start shopping for a place to support your gardening habits, though, narrow down the options by taking a hard look at your construction skills. There are basically four ways to purchase a shed: ready-made structures (some that are delivered in one piece to your backyard); kits where the wood (or metal or vinyl) is precut and all the materials are included; plans that guide you in purchasing materials and building it yourself; or a custom design.

Garden sheds have been adapted from most architectural styles, so you can choose one that mimics or complements your house style. To make sure your mini house is nestled comfortably into its site, consider scale as well as style. A shed that's too big will look out of place and cut into a yard's usability. Small yards can still make way for a simple structure that serves as a focal point for landscaping. Plant in layers around the building's exterior to make the shed a more integral part of your landscape.

Once you decide how it gets built, think about how you need it to function. Will storage of garden tools be its main purpose, or do you need to work in counter space for planting and other outdoor projects? You might want to work in windows and skylights for starting plants. Or carve out space for a sitting area when you're ready to take a break.

RIGHT This narrow garden shed is well suited for stacking long tools or hanging odds and ends. It acts as a colorful pillar to distract the eye away from the privacy fencing behind it.

BELOW Nestled into a knoll of mounding penstemon, lavender, and a creeping rosemary, this shed is a charming multitasker. Its architectural details link it to the main house, which sits only a few feet away.

ABOVE Place a potting shed where it can serve as a garden focal point. This structure is sited at the end of the garden's grassy center pathway to lead the eye through the gardens and let it settle on something charming—and functional.

ABOVE Customize a simple shed plan or kit with siding and trim that draw from your home's design. This potting shed looks charming clad in cedar shakes and shutters. An extra-wide door makes storage easier.

more about...
PLANNING THE RIGHT GARDEN SHED

- **At a minimum**, a garden shed needs to be 3 feet deep for storage.

- **Shelves increase storage flexibility**, but should be at least 13 inches deep to be effective.

- **To improve access**, consider double doors. If you're short on space, consider double doors that slide back across the front of the building instead of swinging out into the yard.

- **If your shed will be used for potting**, work in a counter or freestanding work area at least 3 feet wide and 2 feet deep inside or outside of the structure. For inside work areas, leave at least 3½ feet of depth to allow you to move around or to bring in a stool or chair. Want to bring in a friend too? Seven feet will buy you space for another seating spot.

- **For the best shed-to-yard proportions**, design a structure that takes up 3 to 5 percent of a back lot measuring less than 3,000 square feet.

sheds and outbuildings

Not ready to commit to a potting shed . . . or maybe you have limited property space? This potting area offers a place to putter close to the house. An attached pergola offers up a sense of enclosure and extra shade.

ABOVE LEFT
Garden sheds often have a sense of whimsy about them, a perfect complement for an effusive garden. This garden studio is made much more enchanting when trimmed with a cutout wooden daisy chain.

ABOVE RIGHT
A beautiful shed doesn't need to be tucked away in a corner of the yard. With its timber frame feel, this outbuilding is practical and handsome.

ABOVE Garden structures layered with decoration earn the title garden folly. Gothic windows and a carved spire mark this little hideaway as a folly, though—unlike most traditional follies that have no purpose by definition—it also serves as a sitting area.

•greenhouses and conservatories

A greenhouse is a close relative of the garden shed. Where a potting shed is typically a place to pot up seedlings and containers, its clearer cousin is for starting up seeds and nurturing plants. Still, the lines between these garden houses are often more blurred than that. A potting shed is a natural place to add sunny-side windows for starting seeds in the early season. Likewise, a bench or table for potting is a common sight in a backyard greenhouse.

Greenhouses can be constructed of a variety of materials. Painted wood is lovely to look at but isn't as rot-resistant as treated cedar or enamel-coated aluminum, so it demands more upkeep. Although many greenhouses still have tempered glass panels, UV-coated polycarbonate (especially twin-walled types) or acrylic panels offer more heat retention and are less apt to break.

When considering buying or building a greenhouse, size is the first consideration. Freestanding greenhouses come as small as 6 feet by 6 feet, though most gardeners are happier with a bit more space for people and plants. Plus, small greenhouses present more problems in controlling temperature fluctuations. You can pick from countless styles and shapes, from elaborate structures that mimic a traditional English conservatory to lean-to designs that attach to a home's exterior.

Conservatories are happy places for plants and people alike. Porch furniture and walls of glass join in this natural, indoor-outdoor setting. The lush plants add a final layer of beauty.

ABOVE Give an existing or custom shed more solar power to turn a potting shed into a mini greenhouse. With its clever, sky-facing bump-out window, this old potting shed now offers ample shelves for seed starting.

ABOVE Lean-to greenhouse additions have better heat retention than stand-alone types because they share one wall with the house. To avoid leaks and condensation drips, make sure you have enough wall height to achieve a 4:12 roof pitch as a minimum, as these owners did by extending the height of the wall.

BELOW The window industry steps up its game each year, designing panes that withstand extreme weather while adding sparkle and style to a house. This bump-out bay features floor to ceiling divided pane windows and French doors that have all the charm of a classic conservatory, especially when crowned with a demilune pergola.

•assuring greenhouse success

Of course, the true test of a greenhouse's success is if plants are happy. Consider these basic requirements for a greenhouse that plants will thrive in:

- **Sunlight.** Position a greenhouse for maximum sunshine. Southern exposure allows light all day, a must for many plants. Morning sunlight is most desirable to allow the plant's food production process to begin early.

- **Ventilation.** Removing heat and humidity in exchange for fresh air through natural and mechanical ventilation will make plants happy. Roof vents combined with side louvers will let hot hair escape, drawing cool currents in through the sides. Exhaust fans should be sized to exchange the total volume of air inside the greenhouse each minute.

- **Water.** Obviously, a good watering system is essential. Hand watering is acceptable for most greenhouse crops if someone is available when the task is at hand. A variety of simple automatic watering systems and mist sprayers is available.

- **Drainage.** Good floor drainage is necessary so rainwater and irrigation water will drain away from the floor. Build the greenhouse above the surrounding ground. Pea gravel is a common choice for greenhouse floors.

- **Heating and cooling.** If you use your growing house during extreme temperatures, consider adding a 220-volt circuit electric heater and a small-package evaporative cooler.

Like a house boiled down to its structural essence, greenhouses present artful shapes in the garden. Now many homeowners are getting creative with these little glass houses, using them as studios, entertainment pavilions, or, as in this case, a teahouse with a view.

LEFT Small greenhouses come with all the bells and whistles the big guys have. Though only 8 feet by 10 feet, this little workhouse has a misting system and a brick foundation for humidity control.

RIGHT Greenhouse kits come in all architectural styles and are ready to assemble on site. This greenhouse is topped with details that recall Tudor style. The steeply pitched roof is ideal for snowy climates.

•gazebos and pavilions

These roofed, open-sided outbuildings are built for relaxation and entertainment, so these functions should guide your shelter's design decisions. First, it helps to define terms.

Generally turret-like in shape, a classic gazebo is marked by an open framework, decorative trim, and a domed roof or cupola. This type of garden house is sited to take advantage of a view . . . and to sit pretty in a garden setting. Gazebos are intimate garden spaces, designed to shelter a few folks at a time.

Pavilions often mimic the lines of a home's architecture, but in its sparest, tent-like form. Usually freestanding, pavilions come in countless sizes but are used mostly for dining, entertaining, and enjoying the outdoors in a sheltered way.

For both structures, know that your garden party place might require a building permit. Before building, check your local building codes. Some codes dictate what kind of foundation you'll need for a permanent structure. In some cases, small structures don't require concrete piers or footings but can be situated on concrete blocks or pressure-treated timbers placed directly on the ground.

Put a new slant on poolside living with a modern pavilion that shelters an outdoor bar and kitchen. Angled for maximum sun blockage, this bar has a water and refrigeration source for serving convenience by the pool.

LEFT Gazebos are built on a foundation and/or pilings to secure the small structure and avoid water from seeping up the side posts to encourage rot. This wooden gazebo is as classic as they come and is battened down to a raised wood deck.

BOTTOM LEFT A pavilion doesn't have to be polished up or traditional. If your yard has a naturalized vibe, gather sticks and stones from the surrounding area, then stack and lash them together in a romantic and useful ode to your inner Gilligan.

BOTTOM RIGHT Classically styled pavilions complement formal architecture and can be scaled up or down to meet a site's specific needs. Elegant entertaining is this family's cup of tea, so they planned a space that would fit a large table.

gallery

party places

Draw on familiar, simple shapes and humble materials to create a party place in step with a casual backyard environment. This kitchen and dining room is based on a simple shed design, executed with cinder blocks and repurposed woods. The closed area is a dressing room for a nearby pool.

ABOVE Even small suburban backyards can host a pool party with the right design. This modern pool and party pavilion is clean and open so that it doesn't block out the rest of the lot.

RIGHT An arbor, slatted fencing, and drapes create an intimate space on the deck. The white color makes the space feel large, yet privacy is attainable thanks to drapes at the ready. The fence that wraps around three sides of this breezy living space like a wainscot adds security and architectural character.

utilitarian structures

● ● ● THERE ARE ALL SORTS OF FUNCTIONAL structures to help you out when you need more space to stash your stuff . . . or even the pup. Sheds of all sizes can wrap around yard tools and outdoor clutter. And if you need room to stash big toys—boats, classic cars, or lawn tractors perhaps—a detached garage could be a worthwhile investment.

Gone are the days when your only option for additional outdoor storage was a flimsy metal shed that most likely looked like a mini barn. Wrap a bit of style around your clutter and you'll quickly forget it's there. Choose from modern shed kits or classic storage structures . . . or just about anything in between.

Versatility is a virtue for these secondary structures, allowing them to grow and change in function as your needs change. A playhouse can become a charming garden shed for instance. Or a single-car garage can be transformed into a hobby or art studio.

Modern storage sheds look cool while hiding needed tools and lawn equipment. This eco-conscious kit comes in pieces to be assembled on-site.

ABOVE Thanks to the new focus on all things fresh and local, there's a new type of utilitarian structure flocking to backyards—charming chicken coops. This mail-order modular coop can hold up to six egg layers and sports a cute shed design.

LEFT Many outbuildings can be reinvented when they have outgrown their original purpose. Sure, this log cabin playhouse is a blast for the kids now, but down the line it will also make a handy storage shed.

• garages

Garages—attached to the house or detached—are the norm in many locales. The convenience of an attached garage to protect us from facing the elements on the way from front seat to front door is something to be grateful for. But there are advantages to detached garages that you might consider. Here are a few:

• Detached garages reduce or even eliminate the garage-dominated façades that many homeowners find unappealing.

• You can set a garage back from the house or at an angle, allowing for interesting courtyards, decks, or patios to be placed close to the residence.

• Though an attached garage costs less to build, thanks to needing one less wall, adding an attached garage to an existing home can overwhelm it.

• It's easier to add living space to a detached garage.

ABOVE Garages can be both classically beautiful and add more living space to boot. With an upstairs apartment and a screened porch, this traditional structure looks especially stately when grounded in formal landscaping that includes rose gardens and plenty of boxwood.

RIGHT Not crazy about the same old stretch of cement driveway demanding too much space from your yard? Check out drivable grass systems made of concrete or plastic squares with mesh baking that are strong enough to support cars.

ABOVE Even garages the size of a barn can look charming with the right design and details. Three separate garage bays and a simple gable do the trick here; the gable adds more living space to a studio carved out of the structure's loft.

ABOVE Simple details can lend architectural style to a garage. Here, the hand-forged handles break up the blank façade of a standard lift-up garage door, though they aren't needed to operate the door. Lights in a similar style complete the early American style.

LEFT This charming, unobtrusive garage sits back from the house and is integrated into the gardens, which wrap around the side of the house and continue out back. The bricked area of the driveway functions as additional entertaining space.

pools and play spaces

● ● ●

WITH PROPER PLANNING, YOUR BACKYARD CAN BE A PRIVATE PLAYGROUND that lures kids of all ages outside. All you have to do is include enough designated places to play, and today you'll find options beyond two of the most popular—pools and playgrounds.

If you've been dreaming of taking the plunge into pool ownership, this chapter will explore what it will take to get there. You might find that there is a pool that fits your budget and site parameters, even if your yard is small or awkwardly shaped. Finding an experienced pool contractor or landscape designer will be your first priority if a backyard pool is at the top of your list.

Of course, pools aren't the only way to have fun. Playhouses, court sports, climbing walls, and tree houses pump up the play factor in yards of all sizes. For younger children, reserving a small, shady grassy area offers the perfect place to explore and play. Add a play set when the kids are ready to swing, climb, and slide, and if it doesn't include a small enclosure, then go all out on a custom playhouse that gives them a place to call their own. Don't forget about big kids, too, when considering your outdoor play options.

Your climate, interests, and checkbook should all be considered when planning the playful side of your backyard. This Austin, Texas, family opted for a small raised pool and spa plus a simple dining pavilion to stir up some fun in their small yard.

planning for a pool

● ● ● BEFORE YOU DIVE IN TOO DEEP, FIND A PRO who will consult with you on costs and construction needs. A pool contractor or landscape designer will help determine the optimal size and placement of a pool based on your site. Shop for a firm that has a lot of experience in landscape and pool design. This technical and complex project is best reserved for seasoned professionals.

Before you meet with an expert, do your homework to learn about current trends and technologies in pool construction, water filtration, and heating systems. Pool professionals should be ready to show many examples of their work, answer your questions and discuss options, and provide references. An experienced pro will be familiar with local building requirements on building and fencing, too.

To make sure you're on the same page in terms of size, shape, materials, and extras (such as fountains, lighting, and covers), put together a scrapbook of Web sites, designs, and pictures to share with your builder.

Think about how you will use your pool. Rectangular pools carve out a timeless look and are ideal for lap swimming or water games. Kidney-shaped pools or other organic shapes will blend more naturally with your landscape and are better for quiet lounging, entertaining, and casual dips. Do you want a zero-entry pool for wading or one with steps that span the length of a side? What about an attached hot tub or swim-up bar? Infinity edge? Start with a wish list, but be prepared to prioritize based on how you envision using the pool.

Decide how your family will make the most of a pool investment before committing. This modern concrete pool features a series of geometric components, including a hot tub, fountain wall, and redwood sunbathing deck, indicating it was designed more for entertaining and visual engagement than for swimming or play.

ABOVE Sometimes, the simplest pool design is the best. This rectangular pool could slip into any backyard setting, from sleek and modern to this shingled country home.

more about...
POOL SAFETY

he U.S. Consumer Product Safety Commission (CPSC) recommends taking measures to prevent children from finding their way to the water when there is no adult supervision. In fact, many municipalities and insurance policies demand certain safeguards. Gates should be self-closing, self-latching, and lockable. For extra protection, consider pool or gate alarms along with anti-entrapment drain covers and a securable pool cover. Everyone using the pool should be taught to swim. Making sure some members of the family are trained in CPR and emergency response is another recommended safety precaution.

BELOW Kidney-shaped or freeform pools create a more organic and casual expression. Flagstone decking and a solid, ivy-draped fence provide natural touches while adding to the safety of the pool area.

design and material choices

● ● ● THE MATERIALS YOU CHOOSE WILL determine your pool design and the budget, so choose carefully.

Concrete and plaster remains the tried-and-true option in pool construction, thanks to its relatively low cost and design flexibility. Gunite is the name for the type of dry concrete generally used in pool building. Stronger than poured concrete (this material and its cousin, Shotcrete, have been used to construct tunnels and culverts for decades), these drier cements are sprayed on. The concrete is shot through a hose into a grid of rebar and then covered with smooth plaster. More flexible than standard poured concrete, this material can be shaped to most custom designs and dyed, studded, or decorated.

Simple pool designs made from poured or sprayed-on concrete won't upstage a lush, outdoor setting. This pool's cement shell is tinted blue to enhance its natural beauty.

LEFT Though it's the most durable pool material, concrete is also surprisingly flexible and can be cast into any shape you dream up. Concrete pools with raised sides are gaining popularity in the backyard landscape.

LEFT Butt one edge of a pool to a wall or structure for dramatic effect. A natural stone retaining wall anchors this pool to its surroundings, making it appear that it's been there forever.

•more materials

Fiberglass pools arrive in one big piece on a flatbed truck and are dropped into an excavated area. Though limited in design and less natural than plaster pools, fiberglass units can last 25 years with the proper maintenance, thanks to their durable, watertight, bacteria-resistant finish.

Vinyl is the most common material for above-ground pools, and vinyl liners are an economical option below ground as well. The most stable systems are set into a concrete footing. The vinyl is wrapped around a frame of wood, plastic, or metal. Though less expensive to construct, be aware that the vinyl liner will need to be replaced within 5 to 7 years and will set you back a few thousand dollars.

No matter which material you choose, the most important decision you will make is in picking the right contractor who has experience in creating the type of pool you want.

LEFT Pea gravel can be mixed with cement for an affordable and effective pool surround. It can be installed by an experienced DIYer and provides slip-proof texture. Here it is combined with blue flagstone for a natural look that nestles easily into blooming perennial beds.

BELOW Above-ground pools get a bad rap . . . at least by swimming pool fans that haven't seen the latest options. Semi-inground pools offer the best of both worlds—a less expensive pool that tucks more discreetly into the landscape.

RIGHT Round pools are designed for a casual cool down or convivial entertaining. This semi-inground pool features a fence and stone surround for added beauty and safety.

FACING PAGE Infinity pools need a catch basin and special pumps, making them the most expensive custom installation but the serene effect of the vanishing edge might make the investment worth it.

• pool extras

Before you finalize your pool design, give careful thought to any extras you want to add. It's far more difficult and costly to retrofit elements such as lights, fountains, and spas than it is to conceive of them as part of the original design.

The biggest decision you'll need to make is whether you want a diving board or a slide included in your design. A deep end will add considerable cost to your excavation bill. For lap pools or recreational pools, a flat depth of 4 to 5 feet is standard.

Fencing should meet your local codes and not detract from the pool's aesthetics.

Most municipalities require fences at least 48 inches high with openings no wider than 4 inches. Vertical slats are best because they prevent climbing. Fine mesh is a newer option for a see-through barrier that doesn't mar your view of the pool.

Alarm systems can be installed in the pool or on fencing and gates. In-pool alarms can be attached to pool walls or can be free-floating.

Safety covers add an important layer of protection. To be considered a safety cover, it must be able to support 485 pounds within a 3-foot diameter.

RIGHT An infinity-edge pool creates a fantastic visual illusion of water blending into the horizon due to one side of the pool built lower than the other. For this peaceful extra, you'll need to pay for an additional ledge and basin that catches the water that spills over the lower wall.

FACING PAGE Built-in hot tubs make it easy to move from cool waters to warm when your body temperature demands it. This raised, circular jetted pool allows for some spillover from the hot tub to pool, but is kept separate for more energy efficiency.

ABOVE The stairs in the corner of this pool have a low pitch, making entering and exiting easy for all ages. The lip at the end hides a motorized pool cover.

LEFT Fountains are springing up in and around pools for both pretty and practical purposes. Positioned next to a covered sitting area, the sights and sounds of the cascading water relax guests while circulating the water to ward off pool bugs.

• water systems and heat options

New technologies make picking a filtration system for your pool more complex, especially since there is some controversy surrounding the adverse health effects of chlorine, the most popular method for sanitizing and oxidizing pool water. Salt-water systems lower the amount of chlorine used but don't eliminate it. (In fact, you'll need to purchase a "chlorine generator" to create your own chlorine for these systems.) Chlorine, added according to instructions, outweighs letting bacteria and other contaminants grow in pool water. The main advantages of a saltwater pool are less time in maintenance and less cost in purchasing chlorine.

The good news is that ultraviolet disinfection systems can reduce the chemical levels in saltwater pools. In these systems, UV rays destroy over 99 percent of the organic matter and pathogens found in pools. The light does the heavy lifting, so chemical use can be reduced by 80 to 90 percent. Using fewer chemicals is good for your family's health—and that of the environment.

Thanks to new and often improved heating systems, the cost of maintaining a pool may be less expensive than you might imagine. Even better, these systems allow you to stretch your swimming season by several weeks, no matter what climate you live in.

Rectangular pools can be easily fitted with an automatic cover that tucks under the pool's coping or the material that finishes off the pool edge. This one unfurls to seal in the water's solar gains from a day of sunshine, lowering the heating bill.

LEFT New heating methods can extend your pool season by weeks without breaking the budget. This flat-roof home presents the perfect spot to install a solar heating system, a resource- and cost-effective system, but one that still requires space for a series of flat panels.

BELOW Today, homeowners are looking for more natural options in pool design and water systems. A natural stone border and recycling waterfall add natural touches to this saltwater pool.

more about...
POOL HEATERS

the type of pool and heating system you choose is affected by the climate you live in and the size of the body of water you're heating. Here's a rundown of what's available to you:

• **Gas heaters** are the most widely used systems for heating a pool. Today's gas-fired heaters offer much higher efficiencies than older models, but the cost of maintaining the proper warmth will be dependent on fuel prices. This system is best for pools that aren't used regularly as it can heat pools in the shortest amount of time and in all climates.

• **Heat pump's** cost more than gas pool heaters, but they cost less to operate and typically last longer than gas models. The heater is efficient as long as the outside temperature is above 45° F.

• **Solar heaters** allow you to cut your heating costs significantly. With the right solar site, this type of heater will allow you to swim in comfortable water despite cool weather. Here's the downside: The collector should be 50 to 100 percent of the pool's size, depending on your climate, which can make it a big element to deal with.

spas and hot tubs

●●● IF THE IDEA OF A REGULAR SOAK IN WARM, swirling waters sounds like the perfect prescription for your aches and stresses, reserve a spot in your landscape plans for a backyard spa or hot tub. There are basically two types of hot pools: manufactured portable hot tubs that are self-contained and inground spas.

Factory-made self-contained hot tubs include all of the equipment needed to get the unit up and running. Typically, these self-contained tubs are installed above ground on a flat, solid surface and are powered by a 220-volt hookup to your home's electrical system. Some homeowners choose to build the jetted tubs into decks or patios, but the design must allow easy access to all of the components for repair or cleaning.

An inground tub is most often a pre-plumbed shell or concrete structure that has external heat and filtration components. Though portable factory-made tubs most often use an electric heater and cartridge type filter, inground spas can be powered by all types of heating and filtration systems.

LEFT Sink a spa into a back deck for a seamless, custom look. Raised decking allows owners to access the unit for maintenance and repair.

BELOW Hot bubbly water can soothe aches, pains, and stresses. For those with limited mobility, a semi-inground spa like this one can be easier to access because users can sit on the ledge and swing their legs in.

FACING PAGE Hot tubs don't have to be hot. For the summer months, many owners turn their soaking pools into plunge pools, perfect for cooling off.

• specialty pools

There is a new, roomier type of spa experience called an exercise pool or swim spa to add to your choices in backyard bathing. This specialty pool includes features and equipment to produce a water flow that lets you swim in place or do resistance training. Like hot tubs, exercise spas can be self-contained or custom-built. At a minimum, they are sized to allow an adult to swim in place unobstructed.

If you want a pool primarily for exercise, consider a space-saving lap pool. Lap pools should be at least 45 feet long (so you don't feel like you're constantly switching directions)

and 8 feet wide (so you can do any stroke without hitting the side walls). A depth of at least 3½ feet will ensure knuckles won't scrape the bottom.

If your climate (or exercise routine) demands cooling off more than heating up, consider a plunge pool. These small, shallow tubs or pools are designed for lounging and wading rather than swimming and exercise and are often topped off with a fountain. Or try a traditional, deep well of water for cold-plunge therapy, used for centuries in Chinese medicine for its therapeutic benefits.

Exercise pools often come complete as a fiberglass unit. This one can be installed inground or semi-inground and is finished with tile coping.

LEFT For a pool that's as pretty to look at as it is to soak in, consider a plunge pool. In this classic courtyard, a small but deep plunge pool adds to the geometric fun and is a perfect companion to a warm soaking pool.

BELOW Lap pools take up only a sliver of space, making them a good choice for small or uneven yards. Smaller is better for the budget, too. This lap pool is filled to the brim, creating a clean and serene, modern look.

•outdoor showers

Outdoor showers aren't just for beachgoers anymore. If you've ever stood in the open air under a steady rain of warm water—or cooled off under a chilly stream—you know how luxurious even a simple outdoor shower can be. Part of the charm of the alfresco shower is in communing with nature while you bathe au naturel. And then there is the practical appeal of a spot to rinse grimy garden hands or even bathe the dog.

An outdoor shower can be as simple as a hose, a showerhead, and an outdoor spigot. Or go all out with hot and cold running water, a custom surround for privacy, and a built-in changing room. It's easiest to tie into the home's hot water system. Or, investigate the new on-demand water heaters that can be used outside in a protected place and deliver hot water in an instant.

An outdoor shower is an excellent companion to pools and spas . . . or a relaxing little extra for any backyard. This wood-framed shower offers the needed privacy for a backyard shower but leaves the top third of the stall open to scoop in a watery view.

LEFT Showers assigned to poolside service can shrug off privacy concerns. This open-air shower rinses swimmers off before and after swimming for the health of both the pool water and the swimmer.

BELOW Tuck a spa pool and outdoor shower into a private corner of your yard to create an everyday resort feel. These homeowners built a two-wall shelter of native limestone and added a stone pool surround to knit their soaking spot to the environment.

pool houses

● ● ● AT THE MOST BASIC, A POOL HOUSE provides swimmers a place to change, relax in the shade, use the washroom, or grab a snack and a beverage. This saves pool guests a trek to the main house and saves your house the wear and tear of wet suits and lots of dripping.

Many homeowners take the concept to the next level, designing a structure that includes an outdoor kitchen or dining pavilion. Some structures could even be designed to serve as four-season guest quarters. As with any other outdoor structure, design one near a pool so that it serves how you live and play in that area. Keep in mind that the design of the structure should fit the scale of your yard and pool and echo the style of your house.

For a pool structure with a more relaxed, open-air style, consider a pavilion or pergola. Open on one or all sides, this type of covered shelter offers a protected and private spot that allows visitors to take a shade break and still soak in the backyard surroundings.

A stately pavilion can add elegance to your pool setting. Fabric softens the heavy stonework and offers shade and privacy during hot summer months.

LEFT Even small poolside chambers can seem like the lap of luxury if appointed with the right elements. A wall-mounted sink makes the most of this pool house's pint-size dimensions; its black marble counter makes an elegant statement.

BELOW Pavilions aren't necessarily permanent structures, which makes them a perfect solution for seasonal fun. With classic dentil trim, this vinyl tent offers durability and washability along with shade and wind protection.

LEFT Borrow architectural elements from the main house for a pool house that looks right at home in your backyard. The columns and porch on this poolside guest house mimic the residence for visual continuity.

backyard games

●●● IF YOU WANT YOUR BACKYARD TO BE THE season's hottest destination, add game spaces—for young and old. Many ideas take more creativity than cash. For youngsters, how about creating a small stretch of sand for beach-inspired fun? Or carefully tend a strip of grass for your own private putting practice. Make a horseshoe pit or create a Bocce court. The idea is to carve out play areas that appeal to all ages and abilities.

Trampolines are still popular play spots in backyards everywhere, thanks to the fun and fitness benefits they offer. New safety features make trampolines less of a hazard, though adult supervision is still the best idea. Shop for springless trampolines and those enclosed in tight netting. Check a trampoline's warranty before you buy to ensure it covers at least 2 years of wear. And be sure to consult your insurance agent for any additional fees.

ABOVE If you like to spend time grooming your turf, consider adding a practice green to your backyard. Two types of turf create an eye-catching pattern that visually enhances this backyard.

LEFT A protected corner of the yard can be the right spot for games of skill. A quick-growing hedge of arborvitae and partial walls keep the wind at bay for table tennis. The wheels on the table allow it to be moved easily in inclement weather.

RIGHT Consider the age of your backyard's regular customers before deciding what play elements to include in your plan. A square of playground sand conjures the excitement of the beach in a small corner of the yard.

• play sets

Play sets have grown up a lot over the years. The sawhorse-shaped, tubular steel swing sets of the past have been replaced by kit and custom models that rival those found on school playgrounds. Climbing walls, swinging bridges, tire swings, fort decks . . . if you and your kids dream it, it can likely be done.

Custom play sets can be designed to work with the specific characteristics of your yard. Three mature trees offer up a rambling, shaded area for the kids to climb and swing on. Slatted vertical railings keep them safe, while a corrugated Plexiglas pitched roof provides protection from bright sun and passing rain showers.

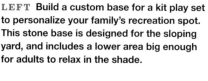

LEFT Build a custom base for a kit play set to personalize your family's recreation spot. This stone base is designed for the sloping yard, and includes a lower area big enough for adults to relax in the shade.

ABOVE Build a little flexibility into areas designed for play so that they morph in function as your family's needs change. This raised pad now holds a rabbit hutch and simple wooden play set, but in a few years it can be converted to a sitting area with a firepit . . . or whatever strikes the owners' fancy.

LEFT Play sets come with an infinite number of happy options for the young ones, including climbing walls and steering wheels. Here, a raised bed of rubber mulch provides 6 inches of padding to prevent injuries from falls.

more about...
HOME PLAYGROUND SAFETY

laying above ground level presents safety concerns, as anyone who's ever skinned a knee or sprained a wrist on a school playground will tell you (and really, who hasn't?). Here are a few ways to minimize the risks on your home turf:

• **Avoid ground that slopes** or is uneven to prevent equipment from slipping.

• **Allow for a 6-foot safety buffer** around equipment, and more for swings. Remove or avoid obstacles such as trees, low branches, fences, large rocks, or concrete.

• **Install a shock-absorbing surface** under your home playground. Grass and dirt don't cut it. Instead, look for rubber mulch (often made out of recycled tires) or rubber playground mats.

• **Cap off any exposed bolts** and close S-hooks so that openings are less than the thickness of a dime.

• **Install guardrails or fencing** around deck areas that are more than 30 inches off the ground.

• court sports

For more elaborate games, consider backyard sport courts. Many pull double duty, for instance, as both a basketball and handball surface. Space will be the biggest consideration, but a small yard doesn't leave you out of the fun. There are game courts and surfaces made for every size yard. One word of warning: Check your neighborhood covenants or local codes that limit the percentage of your yard that contains an impermeable surface. Though cement is typically the base used for game courts, you can also use compacted material (limestone, recycled concrete, etc.) that will be less expensive and less permanent.

ABOVE Full- and half-size basketball courts now dot the suburban landscape. Most courts start with a poured cement pad that is covered with surface tiles that mark the court and provide shock absorption.

LEFT Sometimes the classic backyard sports are the best. Placed on a crushed gravel pad, this tether ball set is perfect for a small California backyard. The flexible surface also becomes a horseshoe pit or croquet court as the mood arises.

Interlocking tiles provide a nonslip, cushioned surface for all types of sports. A switch in tiles converts this basketball court to a field hockey game—and back again—in no time. High mesh fencing keeps all the balls in play.

• playhouses

Playhouses make charming additions to the backyard landscape. Made of wood or plastic, there are designs suitable for all ages. Pick from playhouse kits or building plans, or have one built to your whims. Before you decide, think long term. If you're investing in an elaborate playhouse for the kids, why not pick a style that can later be converted to a garden shed, a guest house, or even a chicken coop. With full-size doors and a ceiling height of at least 7 feet, your tiny house can be a permanent feature of the landscape rather than a short-term fling.

Tiny houses are a bright spot in the landscape; it's just hard not to smile at a little domicile built for pretend. Give the kids a sense of ownership by letting them pick the color palette.

• tree houses

A tree house is a romantic notion—an enchanting hideaway that's as popular with adults as it is with kids. If you're lucky enough to have a tree house–worthy tree, invest in quality materials to keep your tree house as strong and sturdy as the tree it rests in. Choose a simple style that blends with the natural, stately beauty of the tree, and you might find reason to hang out there even when the kids have grown.

There are thousands of tree house plans available, and many are free for the using. If you're handy, consider a kit. Or design your own hideaway. Do plan to call your insurance company before you build as you'll likely need to add to your policy to cover injuries due to use of this soaring structure.

Most tree houses are built into the tree with additional posts that also secure the structures to the ground. But these owners found the perfect spot to attach the little clapboard structure to strong limbs. For more fun and stability, one limb rises through the house.

A treehouse that fits into the nooks and crannies of a faithful old tree is a fantasy no matter what your age. Designer and artist Barbara Butler takes the dream to the next level in colorful custom and pre-designed tree houses and play structures.

more about...
BUILDING A SAFE AND STURDY TREE HOUSE

follow these guidelines when building a tree house. You should also consult your local building department to inquire about necessary permits or restrictions:

• **Choose a strong**, sturdy tree for the tree house.

• **Build the tree house low to the ground.** A tree house higher than 10 feet in the air is too high.

• **Do not build near electrical wires.** A child might try to grab them or swing from them.

• **Surround the area below** the tree house with a protective surface, such as rubber or wood mulch. Use at least 9 inches of protective surfacing in a 5-foot zone around the structure to reduce the shock of a fall.

• **Plan a safe way to get up and down** the tree house. Avoid ropes (including the classic rope ladder) or chains due to strangulation hazards.

• **Use solid barrier walls** around the tree house decking at least 38 inches in height.

• **Check the tree house often** to ensure it's free of dangerous materials such as exposed nails or broken glass.

• **Adult supervision is recommended.** Children younger than 6 years of age should never play in a tree house unless an adult is present.

resources

American Society of Landscape Architects
636 Eye St. NW
Washington, DC 20001-3736
202-898-2444
www.asla.org

The Arbor Day Foundation®
100 Arbor Ave.
Nebraska City, NE 68410
888-448-7337
www.arborday.org

The Association of Pool and Spa Professionals®
2111 Eisenhower Ave.
Suite 500
Alexandria, VA 22314-4695
703-838-0083
www.apsp.org

Capital Landscaping
5465 N.W. 1st St.
Des Moines, IA 50313
515-244-2724
www.capitallandscaping.com

Colorado State University Extension
Campus Delivery 4040
Fort Collins, CO 80523-4040
970-491-6281
www.ext.colostate.edu

Fine Gardening
63 South Main St., PO Box 5506
Newtown, CT 06470-5506
203-426-8171
www.finegardening.com

Iowa State University Extension and Outreach
2150 Beardshear Hall
Ames, IA 50010-2046
800-262-3804
www.yardandgarden.extension.iastate.edu

Lady Bird Johnson Wildflower Center
4801 La Crosse Ave.
Austin, TX 78739
512-232-0100
www.wildflower.org/plants/

National Association of Home Builders®
1201 15th St. NW
Washington, DC 20005
800-368-5242
www.nahb.org

National Gardening Association
237 Commerce St.
Suite 101
Williston, VT 05495
802-863-5251
www.garden.org

North American Deck and Railing Association®
PO Box 829
Quakertown, PA 18951
215-679-4884
www.nadra.org

Sunbrella Fabrics
1831 North Park Ave.
Glen Raven, NC 27217-1100
www.sunbrella.com

U.S. Consumer Product Safety Commission
4330 East West Hwy.
Bethesda, MD 20814
301-504-7900
www.poolsafely.gov

U.S. Department of Agriculture
Natural Resources Conservation Service
Plants Database
www.plants.usda.gov

USDA hardiness zone map

The zones stated in this book are based on several sources and should be treated as general guidelines when selecting plants for your garden. Many other factors may come into play in determining healthy plant growth. Microclimates, wind, soil type, soil moisture, humidity, snow, and winter sunshine may greatly affect the adaptability of plants. For more information and to zoom in on your area, visit the map online at www.usna.usda.gov/Hardzone/ushzmap.html.

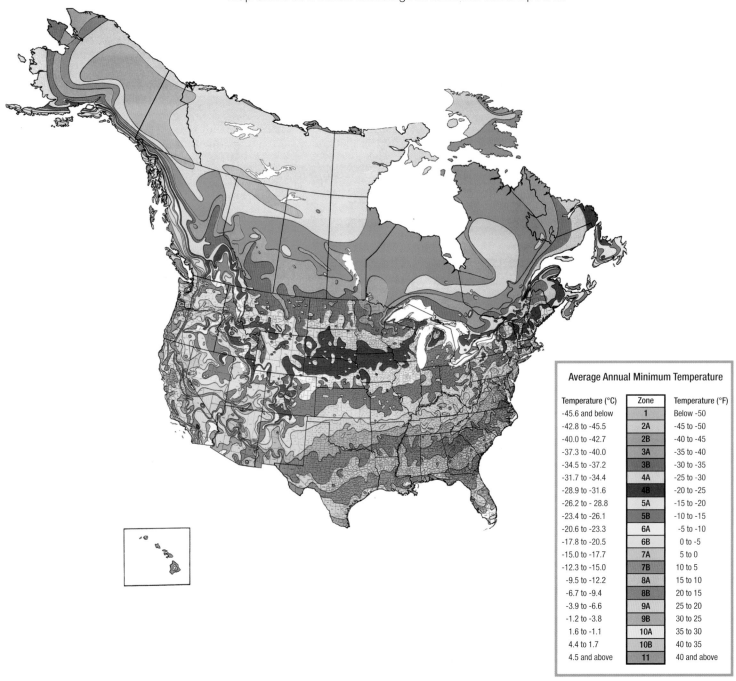

Average Annual Minimum Temperature

Temperature (°C)	Zone	Temperature (°F)
-45.6 and below	1	Below -50
-42.8 to -45.5	2A	-45 to -50
-40.0 to -42.7	2B	-40 to -45
-37.3 to -40.0	3A	-35 to -40
-34.5 to -37.2	3B	-30 to -35
-31.7 to -34.4	4A	-25 to -30
-28.9 to -31.6	4B	-20 to -25
-26.2 to -28.8	5A	-15 to -20
-23.4 to -26.1	5B	-10 to -15
-20.6 to -23.3	6A	-5 to -10
-17.8 to -20.5	6B	0 to -5
-15.0 to -17.7	7A	5 to 0
-12.3 to -15.0	7B	10 to 5
-9.5 to -12.2	8A	15 to 10
-6.7 to -9.4	8B	20 to 15
-3.9 to -6.6	9A	25 to 20
-1.2 to -3.8	9B	30 to 25
1.6 to -1.1	10A	35 to 30
4.4 to 1.7	10B	40 to 35
4.5 and above	11	40 and above

photo credits

FRONT MATTER

p. ii-iii: © Eric Roth, design: robinkramergardendesign.com

p. v: © Mark Lohman

p. vi-1: © Tria Giovan; © Eric Roth, design: www.shconstruction.com; © Eric Roth, design: lombardidesign.com; © Ryann Ford, design: Austin Outdoor Design, www.austinoutdoordesign.com, styling by Adam Fortner, www.creativeandsons.com (top row, left to right); © Eric Roth; © Ryann Ford, design: styling by Adam Fortner, www.creativeandsons.com (bottom row, left to right)

p. 2-3: © Ryann Ford, design: Austin Outdoor Design, www.austinoutdoordesign.com, styling by Adam Fortner, www.creativeandsons.com; © Eric Roth, design: miskovskylandscaping.com; © Eric Roth (left to right)

CHAPTER 1

p. 4: © Tria Giovan

p. 5: © Eric Roth; © Tria Giovan; © Ryann Ford, design: Austin Outdoor Design, www.austinoutdoordesign.com, styling by Robin Finlay, www.voorhes.com; © Tria Giovan (top to bottom)

p. 6: © Ryann Ford, design: Austin Outdoor Design, www.austinoutdoordesign.com, styling by Adam Fortner, www.creativeandsons.com

p. 7: © Ryann Ford, design: Austin Outdoor Design, www.austinoutdoordesign.com, styling by Adam Fortner, www.creativeandsons.com (top); © Eric Roth (bottom)

p. 8: © Ryann Ford, design: B Jane Gardens, www.bjanegardens.com, styling by Robin Finlay, www.voorhes.com (top); © Eric Roth, design: www.christinetuttle.com (bottom)

p. 9: © Eric Roth

p. 10: © Mark Lohman

p. 11: © Eric Roth (top); © Eric Roth, design: lombardidesign.com (center); © Doug Smith (bottom)

p. 12: © Mark Lohman

p. 13: © Tria Giovan (top left); © Eric Roth (top right); © Eric Roth, design: lombardidesign.com (bottom)

p. 14: © Ryann Ford, design: Austin Outdoor Design, www.austinoutdoordesign.com, styling by Robin Finlay, www.voorhes.com (top); © Mark Lohman (bottom)

p. 15: © Ryann Ford, design: Robert Jackson & Michael McElhaney Architects, L&R Landscape Services (left); © Ryann Ford, design: Austin Outdoor Design, www.austinoutdoordesign.com, styling by Adam Fortner, www.creativeandsons.com (right)

p. 16: © Ryann Ford, design: Robert Jackson & Michael McElhaney Architects, L&R Landscape Services

p. 17: © Ryann Ford, design: James David, www.davidpeesedesign.com, styling by Helen Thompson, www.seeninhouse.com (top); © Ryann Ford (bottom)

p. 18: © Eric Roth, design: robinkramergardendesign.com

p. 19: © Mark Lohman (top); © Eric Roth (bottom left); © Tria Giovan (bottom right)

p. 20: © Eric Roth (top); © Eric Roth, design: www.whitlabrothers.com (bottom)

p. 21: © Eric Roth, design: www.horstbuchanan.com (top); © Tria Giovan, design: Designer-Phillip Sides (bottom)

p. 22: © Mark Lohman, design: Barclay Butera Home

p. 23: © Eric Roth

p. 24: © Eric Roth, design: www.spacecraftarch.com

p. 25: © Eric Roth, design: lombardidesign.com

p. 26: © Ryann Ford, design: Austin Outdoor Design, www.austinoutdoordesign.com, styling by Adam Fortner, www.creativeandsons.com

p. 27: © Eric Roth

p. 28: © Ryann Ford, design: Austin Outdoor Design, www.austinoutdoordesign.com, styling by Adam Fortner, www.creativeandsons.com

p. 29: © Eric Roth (top); © Eric Roth, design: ICON Group (bottom)

p. 30: © Eric Roth

p. 31: © Tria Giovan (top); © Eric Roth, design: miskovskylandscaping.com (bottom)

p. 33: © Ryann Ford, design: James David, www.davidpeesedesign.com, styling by Helen Thompson, www.seeninhouse.com (top left); © Mark Lohman (top right); © Tria Giovan (bottom)

p. 34: © Ryann Ford, design: Mell Lawrence Architects, www.architecturalpolka.com, landscape design: www.davidpeesedesign.com

p. 35: © Ryann Ford, design: B Jane Gardens, www.bjanegardens.com, styling by Robin Finlay, www.voorhes.com

CHAPTER 2

p. 36: © Eric Roth, design: www.shconstruction.com

p. 37: © Eric Roth, design: www.greencos.com; © Eric Roth, design: www.poore-co.com; © Ryann Ford, design: Texas Construction Company, www.txconstruct.com; © Eric Roth (top to bottom)

p. 38: © Mark Lohman

p. 39: © Doug Smith (left); © Eric Roth (right)

p. 40: © Eric Roth

p. 41: © Doug Smith (top); © Eric Roth (bottom left and bottom right)

p. 42: © Eric Roth, design: www.greencos.com (top); Charles Bickford, courtesy *Fine Homebuilding* magazine, © The Taunton Press, Inc. (bottom)

p. 43: © Ryann Ford, desigin: Austin Outdoor Design, www.austinoutdoordesign.com, styling by Adam Fortner, www.creativeandsons.com (top); © Eric Roth (bottom)

p. 44: © Mark Lohman, design: Janet Lohman Garden Design (top); © Eric Roth, design: bkarch.com (bottom)

p. 45: © Eric Roth (left); © Doug Smith (right)

p. 46: © Eric Roth, design: treehousedesigninc.com (left); © Eric Roth (top right); © Eric Roth, design: www.lda-architects.com (bottom right)

p. 47: © Eric Roth, design: www.greencos.com (top); © Eric Roth, design: www.spacecraftarch.com (bottom)

p. 48: © Eric Roth, design: Abby Yozell LLC

p. 49: © Eric Roth, design: www.poore-co.com (top left); © Doug Smith (bottom left); © Eric Roth (right)

p. 50: © Eric Roth, design: www.bilowzassociates.com (left); © Eric Roth, design: robinkramergardendesign.com (right)

p. 51: © Eric Roth, design: www.susansargent.com

p. 52: © Eric Roth (top); © Eric Roth, design: treehousedesigninc.com (bottom)

p. 53: © Eric Roth, design: www.baypointbuilderscorp.com (left); © Tria Giovan, design: John Bjornen (top right); © Doug Smith (bottom right)

p. 54: © Eric Roth

p. 55: © Mark Lohman (left); © Tria Giovan (top right); © Doug Smith (bottom right)

p. 56: © Doug Smith

p. 57: © Eric Roth (top left); © Ryann Ford, design: James David, www.davidpeesedesign.com; styling by Helen Thompson, www.seeninhouse.com (bottom left); © Eric Roth (right)

p. 58: © Eric Roth (left); © Doug Smith (right)

p. 59: © Eric Roth

p. 60: © Eric Roth

p. 61: © Mark Lohman, design: Janet Lohman Garden Design (left); © Eric Roth (top right); © Mark Lohman (bottom right)

p. 62: © Eric Roth, design: www.robinkramergardendesign.com

p. 63: © Doug Smith (top left); © Eric Roth, design: www.katherinefield.com (bottom left); © Doug Smith (right)

p. 64: © Eric Roth, design: www.shconstruction.com (left); © Eric Roth, design: www.katherinefield.com (top right); © Eric Roth, design: www.miskovskylandscaping.com (bottom right)

p. 66: © Doug Smith

p. 67: © Mark Lohman (top left); © Ryann Ford, design: Texas Construction Company, www.txconstruct.com (bottom left); © Doug Smith (bottom right)

CHAPTER 3

p. 68: © Eric Roth, design: lombardidesign.com

p. 69: © Jack Coyier, design: Landscape Architecture by Nord Eriksson of EPTDESIGN, Pasadena, CA, www.eptdesign.com; © Ryann Ford, design: styling by Adam Fortner, www.creativeandsons.com; © Tria Giovan; © Eric Roth, design: www.miskovskylandscaping.com (top to bottom)

p. 70: © Jack Coyier, design: ALD Landscape, Santa Monica, California, info@aldco.com

p. 71: © Jack Coyier, design: Pamela Burton & Company Landscape Architecture, www.pamelaburtonco.com (top); © Jack Coyier, design: ALD Landscape, Santa Monica, California, info@aldco.com (bottom)

p. 72: © Mark Lohman

p. 73 © Doug Smith (top); © Tria Giovan, design: John Bjornen (bottom)

p. 74: © Tria Giovan

p. 75: © Eric Roth, design: www.hutkerarchitects.com (top); © Eric Roth, design: www.poore-co.com (bottom)

p. 76: © Doug Smith

p. 77: © Ryann Ford (top left); © Doug Smith (bottom left); © Jack Coyier, design: Artecho Architecture + Landscape Architecture; Pamela Palmer, Landscape Architect, Venice, CA (right)

p. 80: © Ryann Ford, design: styling by Adam Fortner, www.creativeandsons.com

p. 81: © Jack Coyier, design: Artecho Architecture and Landscape Architecture, Venice, CA (top); © Jack Coyier, design: ALD Landscape, Santa Monica, California, info@aldco.com (bottom)

p. 82: © Ryann Ford, design: James David, www.davidpeesedesign.com, styling by Helen Thompson, www.seeninhouse.com

p. 83: © Jack Coyier, design: Artecho Architecture and Landscape Architecture, Venice, CA (top); © Ryann Ford, design: styling by Adam Fortner, www.creativeandsons.com (bottom left); © Mark Lohman (bottom right)

p. 84: © Eric Roth, design: www.kl-la.com

p. 85: © Ryann Ford, design: Austin Outdoor Design, www.austinoutdoordesign.com, styling by Adam Fortner, www.creativeandsons.com (left); © Ryann Ford, design: styling by Adam Fortner, www.creativeandsons.com (top right); © Doug Smith (bottom right)

p. 86: © Ryann Ford, design: Austin Outdoor Design, www.austinoutdoordesign.com, styling by Robin Finlay, www.voorhes.com

p. 87: © Eric Roth (left); © Jack Coyier, design: Landscape Architecture by Nord Eriksson of EPTDESIGN, Pasadena, CA, www.eptdesign.com (right)

p. 88: © Tria Giovan

p. 89: © Eric Roth, design: miskovskylandscaping.com

p. 90: © Doug Smith

p. 91: © Eric Roth, design: miskovskylandscaping.com (top and bottom)

p. 92: © Tria Giovan

p. 93: © Doug Smith (left); © Ryann Ford, design: styling by Adam Fortner, www.creativeandsons.com (right)

p. 94: © Mark Lohman

p. 95: © Doug Smith (top); © Eric Roth (bottom)

p. 96: © Doug Smith (left and right)

p. 97: © Doug Smith (top); © Eric Roth, design: miskovskylandscaping.com (bottom)

CHAPTER 4

p. 98: © Ryann Ford, design: Austin Outdoor Design, www.austinoutdoordesign.com, styling by Adam Fortner, www.creativeandsons.com

p. 99: © Eric Roth; © Eric Roth; © Mark Lohman, design: Janet Lohman Garden Design; © Jack Coyier, design: Artecho Architecture and Landscape Architecture, Venice, CA (top to bottom)

p. 100: © Jack Coyier, design: Environmental Design Studio; www.seanfemrite.com

p. 101: © Jack Coyier, design: Debora Carl Landscape Design, Encinitas CA, info@deboracarl.com (top left); © Ryann Ford, design: B Jane Gardens, www.bjanegardens.com, styling by Robin Finlay, www.voorhes.com (bottom left); © Eric Roth (right)

p. 102: © Lee Anne White, design: Red Rock Pools & Spas

p. 103: © Ryann Ford, design: styling by Adam Fortner, www.creativeandsons.com (left, top right, bottom right)

p. 104: © Ryann Ford, design: Austin Outdoor Design, www.austinoutdoordesign.com, styling by Adam Fortner, www.creativeandsons.com

p. 105: © Ryann Ford, design: Austin Outdoor Design, www.austinoutdoordesign.com, styling by Adam Fortner, www.creativeandsons.com (top); © Eric Roth, design: www.shconstruction.com (bottom)

p. 106: © Tria Giovan

p. 107: © Ryann Ford, design: Austin Outdoor Design, www.austinoutdoordesign.com, styling by Adam Fortner, www.creativeandsons.com (top left); © Tria Giovan (top right); © Eric Roth (bottom)

p. 108: © Eric Roth (top); © Mark Lohman (bottom)

p. 109: © Eric Roth (top left and bottom left); © Mark Lohman (right)

p. 110: © Mark Lohman

p. 111: © Mark Lohman (top); © Mark Lohman, design: Barclay Butera Home (bottom)

p. 112: © Ryann Ford, design: Texas Construction Company, www.txconstruct.com

p. 113: © Mark Lohman (top); © Tria Giovan, design: DesignerJohn Bjornen (bottom)

p. 114: © Mark Lohman, design: Janet Lohman Garden Design

p. 115: courtesy of Sunbrella Fabrics (left); © Tria Giovan, design: Phillip Sides (right)

p. 116: © Ryann Ford, design: styling by Adam Fortner, www.creativeandsons.com

p. 117: © Eric Roth (top); Jennifer Brown, courtesy of *Fine Gardening* magazine, © The Taunton Press, Inc. (bottom left); © Eric Roth (bottom right)

p. 118: © Jack Coyier, design: Artecho Architecture and Landscape Architecture, Venice, CA (top); © Ryann Ford, design: Austin Outdoor Design, www.austinoutdoordesign.com, styling by Adam Fortner, www.creativeandsons.com (bottom)

p. 119: © Jack Coyier, design: architect: form, environment, research (fer) studio L.L.P., Inglewood, CA, www.ferstudio.com; structural engineer: JN Engineering, Los Angeles, CA, www.jnengineering.com; construction manager: Miller and Sons Construction Specialist, Glendale, CA (top); © Jack Coyier, design: Artecho Architecture and Landscape Architecture, Venice, CA (bottom)

p. 120: © Mark Lohman

p. 121: © Ryann Ford, design: B Jane Gardens, www.bjanegardens.com, styling by Adam Fortner, www.creativeandsons.com (left); © Jack Coyier, design: Artecho Architecture and Landscape Architecture, Venice, CA (right)

p. 122: Michelle Gervais, courtesy of *Fine Gardening* magazine, © The Taunton Press, Inc. (top left); © Doug Smith (top right); © Eric Roth, design: robinkramergardendesign.com (bottom)

p. 123: © Doug Smith (left, top right, bottom right)

p. 124: © Doug Smith (left and right)

p. 125: Danielle Sherry, courtesy of *Fine Gardening* magazine, © The Taunton Press, Inc. (top); © Jack Coyier, design: Debora Carl Landscape Design, Encinitas CA, info@deboracarl.com (bottom)

p. 126: © Doug Smith (top); © Jack Coyier, design: Artecho Architecture and Landscape Architecture, Venice, CA (bottom)

p. 127: © Mark Lohman (top left and bottom left); © Lee Anne White (top right); © Doug Smith (bottom right)

CHAPTER 5

p. 128: © Eric Roth

p. 129: © Eric Roth; © Doug Smith; © Eric Roth; © Eric Roth, design: www.hutkerarchitects.com (top to bottom)

p. 130: © Tria Giovan

p. 131: © Mark Lohman (top); © Eric Roth (bottom)

p. 132: Antonio Reis, courtesy of *Fine Gardening* magazine, © The Taunton Press, Inc. (top); Danielle Sherry, courtesy of *Fine Gardening* magazine, © The Taunton Press, Inc., (bottom)

p. 133: © Eric Roth (left); © Eric Roth, design: dressingroomsdesign.com (right)

p. 134: © Eric Roth, design: www.hutkerarchitects.com

p. 135: © Mark Lohman (top left); courtesy of *Fine Homebuilding* magazine, © The Taunton Press, Inc. (top right); © Eric Roth (bottom)

p. 136: © Ryann Ford, design: B Jane Gardens, www.bjanegardens.com, styling by Robin Finlay, www.voorhes.com

p. 137: © Eric Roth, design: Lynda Sutton (top left); © Eric Roth (top right); © Eric Roth (bottom)

p. 138: © Eric Roth

p. 139: © Jack Coyier, design: Richard Krumwiede, landscape architect: Architerra Design Group, Rancho Cucamonga, CA, rkrumwiede@ architerradesigngroup.com (top); courtesy of Sturdi-built Greenhouse Manufacturing Co. (bottom)

p. 140: © Ryann Ford, design: B Jane Gardens, www.bjanegardens.com, styling by Robin Finlay, www.voorhes.com

p. 141: © Mark Lohman (top); © Eric Roth, design: miskovskylandscaping.com (bottom left); © Eric Roth, design: katherinefield.com (bottom right)

p. 142: © Ryann Ford, design: styling by Adam Fortner, www.creativeandsons.com

p. 143: © Ryann Ford, design: styling by Adam Fortner, www.creativeandsons.com (top); © Tria Giovan, design: Phillip Sides

p. 144: Dominic Arizona Bonuccelli, courtesy of Modern-Shed, Inc.

p. 145: courtesy of Williams-Sonoma (top); © Mark Lohman (bottom)

p. 146: © Eric Roth, design: www.jaxtimer.com (left); © Mark Lohman (right)

p. 147: © Doug Smith (top left); © Susan Teare (bottom left); © Doug Smith (top right and bottom right)

CHAPTER 6

p. 148: © Ryann Ford, design: styling by Adam Fortner, www.creativeandsons.com

p. 149: © Lee Anne White, design/build: Robert Nonemaker, Outer Spaces, Inc.; © Eric Roth, design: katherinefield.com; © Jack Coyier, design: Debora Carl Landscape Design, Encinitas CA, info@deboracarl.com; © Jack Coyier, design: Richard Krumwiede, landscape architect: Architerra Design Group, Rancho Cucamonga, CA, rkrumwiede@ architerradesigngroup.com (top to bottom)

p. 150: © Jack Coyier, design: Environmental Design Studio; www.seanfemrite.com

p. 151: © Eric Roth, design: www.kl-la.com (top); © Mark Lohman, design: Janet Lohman Garden Design (bottom)

p. 152: © Mark Lohman

p. 153: © Lee Anne White, design: Red Rock Pools & Spas (top); © Eric Roth, design: www.bilowzassociates.com (bottom)

p. 154: © Eric Roth

p. 155: Lee Anne White, design/build: Robert Nonemaker, Outer Spaces, Inc. (top left); Ken Southam, Vancouver, BC, courtesy of Endless Pools (top right); © Lee Anne White, design/build: Jamie Scott/Groupworks (bottom)

p. 156: © Eric Roth

p. 157: © Ryann Ford, design: Austin Outdoor Design, www.austinoutdoordesign.com, styling by Adam Fortner, www.creativeandsons.com (top); © Lee Anne White, design: Red Rock Pools & Spas (bottom left); © Eric Roth, design: www.shconstruction.com (bottom right)

p. 158: © Jack Coyier

p. 159: © Eric Roth, design: www.christofiinteriors.com (left); © Eric Roth (right)

p. 160: © Mark Lohman, design: Barclay Butera Home

p. 161: © Jack Coyier, design: Artecho Architecture + Landscape Architecture; Pamela Palmer, Landscape Architect, Venice, CA (top); © Eric Roth, design: katherinefield.com (bottom)

p. 162: © Jack Coyier, design: Artecho Architecture + Landscape Architecture Pamela Palmer, Landscape Architect; Venice, CA

p. 163: © Tria Giovan (top); © Mark Lohman

p. 164: © Eric Roth, design: treehousedesigninc.com

p. 165: © Ryann Ford, design: B Jane Gardens, www.bjanegardens.com, styling by Robin Finlay, www.voorhes.com (top and bottom)

p. 166: © Lee Anne White, design/build: Robert Nonemaker, Outer Spaces, Inc.

p. 167: © Ryann Ford (top left); © Tria Giovan, design: Designer John Bjornen (top right); © Lee Anne White, design/build: Jamie Scott/Groupworks (bottom)

p. 168: © Mark Lohman

p. 169: © Lee Anne White, design: Red Rock Pools & Spas (top); © Jack Coyier, design: Debora Carl Landscape Design, Encinitas CA, info@deboracarl.com (right)

p. 170: © Ryann Ford, design: styling by Adam Fortner, www.creativeandsons.com (top and bottom)

p. 171: © Jack Coyier, design: Richard Krumwiede, Landscape Architect, Architerra Design Group, Rancho Cucamonga, CA, rkrumwiede@ architerradesigngroup.com (top left); © Jack Coyier, design: Landscape Architecture by Nord Eriksson of EPTDESIGN, Pasadena, CA, www.eptdesiign.com (bottom left); © Mark Lohman (right)

p. 172: © Mark Lohman

p. 173: © Ryann Ford, design: styling by Adam Fortner, www.creativeandsons.com (left); © Mark Lohman (right)

p. 174: © Mark Lohman

p. 175: © Mark Lohman (left); © Lee Anne White, design: Hillary Curtis, David Thorne Landscape Architect (right)

p. 176: © Ryann Ford, design: styling by Adam Fortner, www.creativeandsons.com

p. 177: Design and Image by Barbara Butler, Barbara Butler Artist-Builder, Inc., 415-864-6840 www.barbarabutler.com

p. 178: © Eric Roth

index

If you like this book, you'll love *Fine Gardening*.